Sexual betrayal

SUCKS,

but you got this.

MOVE THROUGH BETRAYAL TRAUMA TO A RESTORED, CONFIDENT YOU

BECKY JONES

ISBN: 978-1-7347641-2-3

Printed in the United States of America.

Cover Design by 100Covers.com
Interior Design by FormattedBooks.com

DOWNLOAD THE AUDIOBOOK FREE!

Just to say thanks for buying my book, I would like
to give you this audiobook 100% FREE!

To download go to:
https://beckyjonesbtcoach.com/freeaudiobook

Dedicated to *you*. Yes, *you*!!

I'm sorry you're here.

If I was there, I would hug you and we'd fall
to the ground and cry together.

Then I would stand up and extend my hand to you.

"It's time to get up. You can't stay here.

You can do this!"

I would walk beside you, step by step, as you start
walking the road to healing from betrayal trauma.

CONTENTS

INTRODUCTION

I f you have been sexually betrayed, you have work to do regardless of what you decide to do with your relationship with that person. Recovery work is now sitting on your lap like a white fluffy lap dog and it'll stay there regardless of whether you stay or leave the person that betrayed you.

In this book, I don't address whether you should leave or stay with the person who sexually betrayed you. What's on the table is the fact that you've been sexually betrayed in your most intimate, personal relationship and *you* have to figure out how to cope and recover from this betrayal.

That's what we're here to do. We're dealing with *you,* not your partner, not your relationship with your partner, but *you.*

And let's be completely honest, when you're dealing with *your* trauma, taking care of yourself, loving yourself, and seeing yourself as you should be seen, in short, working your recovery, well, that's the space that will lead you to the healthiest decisions about what to do with the relationship that put you here to begin with. When you're in that beautiful place of recovery, you're not stopped by false views about who you are. You'll know what you need. In that space of recovery, what to do with that relationship will be an unforced decision that you'll naturally step into.

Until then, we have some work to do.

Sexual betrayal sucks, but you got this!!

MY STORY

It was 4am when my husband's cell phone rang. My body rolled over as I felt him jump out of bed and grab his phone. My eyes blinked repeatedly to try to focus on my husband's silhouette as he left the room to answer the phone.

This day my world turned upside down. The foundational rug that I thought was my life was pulled out from underneath me with a jerk.

This was the day that I started to walk the rocky road of healing from betrayal trauma.

I want to compare healing from betrayal trauma to walking down a rocky road in bare feet. If you try doing that, it wouldn't be long before you start cursing those tiny rocks you're trying to walk on.

The road of healing from betrayal trauma is a very rocky road. The road is riddled with large dark rocks, jagged brown rocks, and some soft and smooth clear rocks. Everywhere I stepped, my bare feet pulled back in pain and I sharply sucked in my breath. The rocks poked at my virgin feet, soft and white, unaccustomed to this type of terrain. I stumbled about, my feet tender and smarting from each last step I took. There was no reprieve as the next step forward only brought more pain as my foot once again stepped on a jagged rock.

Angrily, I crouched down, picked up the rocks, and started throwing them far from me. It felt good. But it was pointless. I was surrounded by rocks. I was surrounded by pain and no relief was in sight. Defeated, I stopped and my legs crumbled beneath me and I sat on the ground cross-legged. I put my face in my hands and started sobbing. My shoulders heaved forward as the pain inside of me starting coming out in huge wailing gulps. I can't do this! It's too much! It's unfair I have to do this, so unfair!

There was a break in my tears and through my soggy, unfocused eyes, I stared at the rocks surrounding me. They weren't rocks at all. They were pebbles. I stroked my hand over the nearest ones and picked them up. My hand cradled beautifully colored pebbles of all shapes and sizes and colors. Some pebbles were pitch black and glossy. Some were white and clear. Some were jagged with multiple shades of earthy hues. The longer I stared at these pebbles the more I didn't hate them. They were no longer my enemy. One by one, I pulled each rock to my face and rubbed it against my cheek.

You're on the same road–different stories but the same road–great pain, loss of hope, fear, not feeling safe, and feeling disconnected from yourself.

An indirect casualty in the sexual betrayal arena is that you've lost connection with yourself. You've disconnected from yourself and don't trust yourself because of someone else's behavior and treatment of you. Betrayal trauma strikes at the cords we relied on for peace and comfort and safety.

Another indirect casualty of sexual betrayal is losing connection and trust in your Higher Power. Even our relationship with our Higher Power is affected. It's hard to trust God. How could He let this happen? Why didn't He stop me from entering this relationship? Like water filling up the air pockets in a sinking submarine, more questions than answers fill our mind. Many drop their religious practices. My intent is to encourage you NOT to do so. My intent is to encourage you to muster all the faith you have and continue forward in your religious practices. Don't drop God. He didn't cause this. One of His children did. Others have their choices and agency to do as they choose. But He has the power to redeem us from the choices of others.

This book is about where I "started" and about the beginning, middle, and "end" of healing from betrayal trauma.

This book is about lessons I've picked up on my road to healing from betrayal trauma. It's about the pebbles I've put in my pocket. These lessons come from a variety of sources: reading books and scriptures, therapists, online courses and classes from betrayal trauma experts, conversations with others going through betrayal trauma, and personal revelation from God.

By committing to work on myself and not staying stuck in my trauma, God hasn't left me alone. I've been given what I needed, hour by hour. God fed me manna day by day, just as He did for the children of Israel.

I'm now a betrayal trauma coach and am helping people all over the world who've been sexually betrayed.

If I were sitting by you, I'd hug you, cry with you, feel with you. I would squeeze you tight and tell you that despite this horrible betrayal that has happened to you, you're loved and you're not alone. I'd look into your tear-filled eyes and confidently tell you that God provided a way for you to escape the destructive choices of another. I'd confidently tell you, "You've got this. You can do this."

My intent as a betrayal trauma coach is to keep you to moving forward. Yes, you'll have days when you say to me, "Becky, I need to sit down. I can go no further."

That's okay. We'll sit down and rest. After a while we'll need to get up and keep walking. We can't sit there forever. This betrayal won't define your life. However, it will be a defining moment IN your life.

In this chapter, we talked about the reality of where you are in your life right now; you've been sexually betrayed. In the next chapter, we'll talk about what betrayal trauma is.

YOUR ACTION PLAN

Journal

- What is your story? Write down what your partner has done to betray you.
- How did you find out about the betrayal? What was your reaction when you found out?
- Did the betrayal affect your relationship with your Higher Power?
- Did the betrayal affect your relationship with yourself?
- What are the consequences if you don't get up and move through this betrayal?

Physical action

- Go into a quiet space, preferably where there's a mirror. Look at yourself in the mirror. As if you were looking at a friend, tell yourself what you found out and what happened. Have the person in the mirror cry with you and tell you how sorry they are that this happened.
- Draw, paint, or mold a piece of art that depicts how you feel right now.

Mental Action

Repeat these affirmations morning and night:

I can heal
God will help me in the pain

For the full list of affirmations, go to
https://beckyjonesbtcoach.com/freeactionguide

WHAT IS BETRAYAL TRAUMA?

had already forgotten about the 4am phone call when my spouse asked to take me for a drive. The pine trees smelled delicious as my spouse and I drove up a dirt road into the mountains. My heart felt happy. The golden light from the mid-morning sun created what seemed would be a great day. It reminded me of that beautiful day, seventeen years earlier, when he drove me into the mountains to ask me to be his wife. But soon, I became unaware of any other sensation except for an extreme pain in my heart, like it had been stabbed, as he divulged sexual betrayal.

I thought I married someone who would step in front of an oncoming truck to save me. Turns out, he was the one driving the truck.

Within a matter of minutes, the person whom I depended on, trusted, and connected with went from a source of companionship and support to a source of pain, fear, and deep uncertainty. I had thought my relationship created a stable platform from which I viewed and operated in the world. That platform was now blown apart.

And there I sat.

You're most likely experiencing betrayal trauma if you have a committed partner who has betrayed you sexually through porn, emotional affairs, physical affairs, online chatting or texting, virtual sex, or one-night stands.

And there you sit.

What is betrayal trauma?

Dr. Jill Manning defines betrayal trauma well on her website.
Trauma is defined as a deeply distressing or
overwhelming experience that is commonly followed
by emotional and physical shock. If left unresolved
or untreated, traumatic experiences can lead to short
and long-term challenges. Examples of traumatic
events include: sudden death of a loved one, physical
or sexual assault, witnessing violence, natural disasters,
car accidents, military combat.

In contrast betrayal trauma occurs when someone we
depend on for survival, or are attached to, violates our
trust in a critical way. Examples of betrayal trauma
include: contracting an STD from a supposedly
faithful partner, discovering evidence of a spouse's
sex addiction, sexual or physical abuse by a parent,
financial deceitfulness in a marriage.

Although betrayal trauma shares many of the
same psychological, physiological and neurological
symptoms associated with fear-based traumas, it is
distinct in two important ways:

The perpetrator is in close relationship with the victim:

Perpetrators of betrayal traumas are in close relationship
with the victim, and therefore the violation of
trust is experienced as a deeply personalized (versus
random) offense.

Because of the personalized nature of the betrayal,
betrayal trauma can be more destabilizing to one's

social schema than a fear-based trauma. Research has also shown betrayal trauma to be associated with more physical illness, anxiety, dissociation and depression than traumas low in betrayal.

For example, a serious car accident may be frightening or even life-threatening, but it would be unusual for a car accident to cause someone to question the legitimacy of a primary relationship. Betrayal trauma jeopardizes the safety of the relationship one would turn to for comfort when distressed, causing extraordinary vulnerability at a time of great need.

High risk of reoccurrence:

Because of the close and interconnected relationship between the perpetrator and the victim, it can be difficult to confront or sever ties with the perpetrator. As a result, victims may feel trapped and remain in the relationship out of necessity, making the risk of future reoccurrence of betrayal trauma higher than with random or accidental traumas.

A person who is physically assaulted by a stranger, for instance, is unlikely to encounter the same aggressor a second time. A betrayed spouse, on the other hand, typically shares a life, home, children, extended family, and finances with the perpetrator. These life ties make extrication infinitely more complex and prolonged — even if the victim divorces the perpetrator."[1]

---

[1] "What Is Betrayal Trauma." Dr. Jill Manning. Accessed February 8, 2020. https://drjillmanning.com/betrayal-trauma/.

Partner Hope, a website for betrayal partners described betrayal trauma.

> It makes you feel like you are losing your mind. It puts you on an emotional rack and pulls you in opposite directions until you are begging for mercy or you break and ricochet over to one extreme just to find relief.

> Every betrayed partner is dealt two blows at once when they discover their spouse's sexual behavior. Blow number one is the gut punch of betrayal; a breathtaking breach in trust that changes your relationship in permanent ways. Blow number two is the shocking realization that your partner has been extravagantly and expertly lying and manipulating reality in order to cover up their behaviors. These blows smash into your heart and in an instant plunge you into a whole new world.

> When I experienced this, in seconds, the person who I depended on and was deeply connected to went from being a source of support and companionship to being a source of pain, fear and deep uncertainty. My relationship, which had created a stable base from which I was able to operate in the world, was suddenly a rickety mess.[2]

Betrayal trauma affects every part of your life: your relationship with your partner, family, friends, your Higher Power, and yourself. You're thrust into a world where you feel extremely unsafe and vulnerable. Like a catastrophic 8.0 earthquake, everything you knew before is destroyed.

How do you move forward as you start down your path to healing from betrayal trauma and putting your world back together again?

---

[2] "Home." Partner Hope. Accessed February 8, 2020. https://partnerhope.com/.

I'll help you.

In this chapter, we talked about what betrayal trauma is. In the next chapter, I'll tell you how this book is laid out.

YOUR ACTION PLAN

Journal:

- What did you know about betrayal trauma before reading this chapter?
- Did a friend or family member experience it?
- What did you think about them or why it happened?
- What were your preconceived notions about betrayal trauma?

Physical Action:

Get on the computer and do a Google search using the search terms "betrayal trauma." What do you see?

Mental Action:

Repeat this affirmation morning and night:

God has a plan for me!

For the full list of affirmations, go to
https://beckyjonesbtcoach.com/freeactionguide

HOW IS THIS BOOK LAID OUT?

This book is laid out in a sequential framework: the beginning, middle, and end of your road to healing from sexual betrayal. In each stage, I describe the lessons that had come to me as I worked to recover from betrayal trauma.

1. The beginning. This stage is when you first find out about the sexual betrayal of your partner. In the industry, it's called "D" day or discovery day. This is the day you start walking your road to heal from betrayal trauma. In the beginning, you're honestly just breathing in and out and trying to manage the deep pain you're in.
2. The middle. This stage is when you're just barely coming up for a breath from the prolonged deep pain that you've been experiencing. You see tiny glimpses of vistas and relief past the all-encompassing place of pain you've been in.
3. The end. There never is an end. But this "end" stage is the beginning of a new road. At this point, you've learned and grown in amazing ways. This growth now provides an amazing framework to allow the beauty of life to shine in and the bad to be kept out with healthy boundaries, disconnecting from lies and toxicity, and dealing with difficult emotions. This is the place where you have a

healthy emotional awareness and regulations, where you can watch your emotions with curiosity and without judgment, where you intimately trust yourself and the truth inside you guides your life.

In this chapter, we discussed how this book is laid out. In the next chapter, we'll talk about what it looks like in the beginning of your road to healing from betrayal trauma.

THE BEGINNING OF YOUR ROAD TO HEAL FROM BETRAYAL TRAUMA

In this chapter, I'll describe how I felt at the beginning of my road to healing from betrayal trauma. Figuratively, I was just hit by a truck. I was taken to the hospital intensive care unit where I was hooked into breathing machines. My face was swollen and bruised from the impact. No skin was exposed because every other part of my body is wrapped in bandages. I went in and out of consciousness from the pain medication that the doctors were giving me. The room was quiet and the nurses and doctors spoke in hushed tones. They weren't sure I was going to make it.

Figuratively, I was in the ER at first and then was moved to the intensive care unit. I was in this critical stage for awhile. In the beginning I did nothing else but breathe in and out, trying to stay alive and manage the intense pain that came from my injuries. I thought nothing about healing or rehabilitation. I thought nothing about life outside of the ER. I only went from moment to moment, breathing in and out and managing the pain.

We'll be focusing on the beginning of your journey right now. The "beginning" is when you first find out about your partner's betrayal. No matter what your betrayal story is, I'm confident you'll come upon these beginning pebbles on your journey.

If you've already gone through the "beginning stage," you may recognize these lessons. It would still benefit you to read this section because it would validate the lessons you may have already picked up.

In this beginning phase, we'll be discussing other people's choices, healing and what it takes, your emotions and how to manage and deal with them, blocking out other people's opinions, validation, feeling safe, fighting back, blame, and finding out what you want.

In this chapter, I illustrated what it looks like being at the beginning of your road to healing from betrayal trauma. In the next chapter, I'll open up my pocket and show you what I put there. No matter what your story is, healing takes work. That's the first pebble I put in my pocket.

YOUR ACTION PLAN

Journal:

- Where would you say that you are on your road to healing?
- Write your expectations of healing and how long you want to be in the "hospital."
- How would you figuratively describe yourself right now? If you can't find the words to describe yourself, draw a picture of how you feel inside.
- What are your abilities at this point? (I could only breathe and manage the pain.)
- What is the extent of your injuries?

Physical Action:

Do some deep breathing exercises to connect with your body. Feel the breath going in and out of your body. That breath was given to you. It was given to you by your Higher Power. Just feel your chest rising and falling with each breath.

Mental Action:

Repeat this affirmation morning and night:

I am strong

For the full list of affirmations, go to
https://beckyjonesbtcoach.com/freeactionguide

HEALING TAKES WORK

In this chapter, I'll highlight three important points: healing takes work, you'll need others to help you, and it's important to seek spiritual gifts.

In the beginning of my journey to heal from betrayal trauma, I was lying in a hospital bed. I was barely alive. I was full of bullet holes, riddled with rounds of lies and a different reality than what I thought I was living in. I was bruised with unfulfilled expectations and bleeding from a broken heart. I was broken because of the lack of commitment in my most important relationship. The bleeding wouldn't stop. I was weak and faint. My breathing was slow and deep because of the huge amounts of trauma and pain I was in. My breath was the only thing I could count on, the only sure thing in my life at that point. Breathing in and out.

At this point in the beginning of my journey of healing from betrayal trauma, someone recommended a website called bloomforwomen.com.[3] It's a website dedicated to helping women heal from betrayal trauma. Bloom for women has online classes, support groups, coaches, and therapists dedicated to helping women heal from betrayal trauma.

I decided to try it.

---

[3] "Homepage." Bloom for Women. Accessed February 8, 2020. https://bloomforwomen.com/.

In one of those classes, the instructor, Dr. Skinner[4], who is a specialist in betrayal trauma, said he has seen people stuck in their trauma for years.

That statement hung in the air like a balloon.

I lowered my gaze and stared at my feet. Shaking my head, I whispered to myself, "I don't want to be in this place. I want to get out as soon as possible."

Dr. Skinner said, "Although someone has hurt you and the last thing on your mind is to get up and work, that is something you must do to heal. Healing takes work."

My fingers reached up to my bowed head, and I sat there just rubbing my eyelids. I noticed I had stopped breathing. I forced my belly to expand, taking in a slow stream of air, long and deep into my body and exhaling it out as a sigh.

Acceptance came in that moment. I was here. I was betrayed. I wasn't a pretty sight.

I couldn't stay in this state. Part of me wanted to stay there as a witness to the world of what this person did to me. That thought left as quickly as it came, as I told myself what a bad idea that was. That would only hurt me.

"But, I don't want to get up and walk this road. It's too hard." I blurted out loud as I wrestled with myself.

"But Becky, if you stay here, you'll die in other ways. Who you are will die. Who God created you to be in this world will die. And then other people's choices and decisions would determine your life, not your choices." The other side of myself was firm and clear. "I know you're hurting. But you can't stay here."

I decided I wouldn't sit by and lick my wounds and feel sorry for myself. I would get up. I wanted to feel better. I wanted to feel less fear. I wanted to feel safe. I wanted to feel loved. I wanted to create safety for myself.

I wasn't sure how I was going to do that, but I promised myself in that moment that every day from here on out, I would lean into the wind

4   "Dr. Dr. Kevin Skinner And Addo Recovery, LMFT, CSAT, EMDR, Marriage & Family Therapist, Lindon, UT, 84042." *Psychology Today.* Sussex Publishers, July 20, 2019. https://www.psychologytoday.com/us/therapists/dr-kevin-skinner-and-addo-recovery-lindon-ut/285636.

and seek after anything that might help me. I committed to 15 minutes a day to study about betrayal trauma, what it was and how people walked through it and navigated it. I committed to at least 5 minutes of journal work where I could dump my feelings and process. I also committed to strengthen my religious practice and do my religious study and prayers morning and night for 15 minutes.

My dad died suddenly at age 57 of a heart attack. I watched as my mom was thrust into a world of intense, suffocating grief at the loss of her dear companion. But I also watched her scoop up the pieces of her broken and shattered heart and press forward. I watched her push aside the temptation to be bitter or angry.

Uncannily, the same year that my dad died, 33 men were trapped 700 meters underground in a collapsed mine in Chile. Two thousand three hundred feet of rock and dirt were on top of them. They couldn't get out on their own.

Grief feels as suffocating as 2,300 feet of rock and dirt on top of me. I needed help. But who could help me? I recognized I couldn't do this on my own. I needed to find people to help me.

I found people a few steps ahead of me in their journey. Their stories helped me. I talked to them and I read what they did.

How can other people help you?

The Sucthat once a month in my church. It's a very strengthening principle that's very useful in my life. Fasting is when I give up food and water for two meals. I focus on God during this time of fasting to draw closer to Him.

On this Sunday, a powerful experience landed in my lap while I was fasting. Looking back, it was an experience to prepare me for what I would soon find out.

I woke up early to read my scriptures, pray, and write in my journal. While pondering, a voice came to my mind. I knew it was God.

He said, "Do you believe that I exist?"

As if I was in a conversation, I replied, "I do."

"Then," God said, "You will seek every gift I have for you."

This experience set the stage to seek God and His spiritual gifts with all my heart. This experience directed me to seek out the gifts that God could give. I would need them to survive.

This experience gave me faith to know that God was there and could bless me to do everything I needed to do.

Somehow, the faith I needed to believe that I *could* be nourished by God came and I leaned on Him every minute. Somehow, God gave me the strength I needed to get up and put one foot in front of the other. I testify that He fed, watered, and strengthened me. I wasn't left alone.

I rubbed both of my hands up and down on my forehead feverishly. "I don't know what I need!" I could feel my heart squeezing underneath the weight of my pain that was magnified under the reality that I didn't know how to take care of myself. My eyes squeezed tight. I guess that's where I would start by asking God what I need. Then, thoughts came into my mind out of nowhere.

What about the gift of peace? What about courage to speak my truth even if I'm afraid? What about faith to continue my religious practices and believe that God is loving despite having this happen to me? What about faith to believe that I'm valuable despite the rejection I received? What about the gift of patience because this is a problem that won't easily be solved? What about the gift of faith to believe God will help me and speak to me and teach me?

I wondered what would happen if I *didn't* seek out these gifts.

A smorgasbord of gifts I needed was presented to me and I was hungry.

I started praying for these gifts.

In this chapter, we talked about how healing takes work, and we must do the work. We also talked about how we would need help from others and from our Higher Power and the spiritual gifts He offers us. In the next chapter, we'll discuss the reality that other people's choices hurt us.

YOUR ACTION PLAN

Journal:

- What time can you devote to healing work for your mind, body and spirit?
- What is holding you back from doing the work to heal? Resources? Desire? People?
- What will die inside you if you stay where you are?
- How can other people help you?
- What gifts do you need?
- What would happen if you don't have those gifts?

Physical Action:

Make a vision board of you: who you are and what your dreams are. Cut out pictures or draw. Are you soft and cuddly like a cat? Do you like horses? Do you have a dream of owning your own business someday? Do you love chocolate?

Put everything about yourself, creatively on a big board and put it by your bed or mirror so you wake up and go to sleep remembering who you are.

Mental Action:

Repeat these affirmations morning and night:

I can be provided for in my want

For the full list of affirmations, go to
https://beckyjonesbtcoach.com/freeactionguide

OTHER PEOPLE'S CHOICES

O ther people's choices will hurt you. If we step outside of our sexual betrayal lens for a moment, we can see how others have been affected in different ways by other people's choices.

Richard Norby[5] was serving a church mission in Belgium. On a certain fateful morning, he took some young missionaries to the airport to drop them off so they could fly home. That same morning, 2 suicide bombers carried out an attack at the Brussels airport that killed 30 people. Luckily he wasn't killed, but he was mangled and severely injured.

This man came and spoke in an evening meeting that my daughter attended. At that meeting, he said something that my daughter repeated to me and that I have never forgotten.

> I don't look down at my scars and feel anger about what
> happened to me. I look down at my scars and remember
> that He saved me.

---

[5] Swensen, Jason. "'He Was in Charge': Richard Norby on Surviving Brussels Bombing through Faith in Jesus Christ." Church News, February 26, 2019. https://www.thechurchnews.com/members/2019-02-26/general-conference-rirchard-norby-terrorist-attacks-on-surviving-brussels-bombing-moving-forward-with-faith-in-jesus-christ-4477.

"Behold, I have graven thee upon the palms of
my hands," [6]

It's humbling to realize that Christ has scars on His
hands because he suffered for me. I imagine that every
time He looks at His palms, He thinks of me, not with
anger that He had to go through what he did but with
love. His heart is filled with love and purpose, for me,
when He looks at His scars.

Stepping back into our betrayal trauma box that we're in, God *knew*
that other people's choices would cause you and me pain. Other people's
choices would change the landscape of our lives. He has a plan for this and
prepared a way for us to be healed and find joy and happiness despite the
destructive choices of others! He has helped countless other people move
healthily through other people's harmful choices.

He sent His Son so that you have the opportunity to escape the destructive choices of another.

He sent His son with Healing in His wings.

He sent His son to sanctify your deepest distress[7]

He sent His Son to pay the debts owed to you.[8]

He sent His Son to show us the path of healing from other people's
choices that hurt us.[9]

"The Spirit of the Lord *is* upon me, because he hath anointed me to
preach the gospel to the poor; he hath sent me to heal the brokenhearted,

[6] "Isaiah 49." The Church of Jesus Christ of Latter-day Saints. Accessed February 8, 2020. https://www.churchofjesuschrist.org/study/scriptures/ot/isa/49?lang=eng.

[7] "How Firm a Foundation." The Church of Jesus Christ of Latter-day Saints. Accessed February 8, 2020. https://www.churchofjesuschrist.org/manual/hymns/how-firm-a-foundation?lang=eng.

[8] Rasband, Ester. *The Promise of the Atonement: Cure for Broken Dreams.* Springville, UT: Cedar Fort, 2005.

[9] Rasband, Ester. *The Promise of the Atonement: Cure for Broken Dreams.* Springville, UT: Cedar Fort, 2005.

to preach deliverance to the captives, and recovering of sight to the blind, to set at liberty them that are bruised,"[10]

I was blind. I couldn't see who was safe. I couldn't see who I was anymore. I couldn't see who God was anymore. I couldn't see that life could hold any more beauty or happiness ahead. I was bruised and bleeding and needed to be set free and healed.

It's my testimony to you that God loves you. God is aware of you. He knows what you're feeling right now. He has provided a way for you to escape the destructive choices of another.

How?

The path of healing will unfold step by step as you learn of Him and seek Him out daily, even hourly. He will speak to you. He will honor you and bless you with the knowledge you need. You can do this. You've got this.

In this chapter, we established the fact that other people's choices hurt us. In the next chapter, we'll talk about what emotions will come up for you when you've been sexually betrayed.

---

[10] "Isaiah 61." The Church of Jesus Christ of Latter-day Saints. Accessed February 8, 2020. https://www.churchofjesuschrist.org/study/scriptures/ot/isa/61?lang=eng.

YOUR ACTION PLAN

Journal:

- What choices have people made in your life that have hurt you?
- Do you have a Higher Power? What do you believe your Higher Power does for you?
- What ways are you poor?
- How are you blind?
- How are you bruised?
- In what ways do you need to be set free?
- What do you need deliverance from?
- What are your daily religious habits? How do you seek out your Higher Power?
- What blessings have you had in the past that help you see His hand in your life?
- How has someone else's Higher Power helped them in their life?

Physical Action:

Is there someone in your life who has made decisions that hurt you? Go into a quiet place. If you're in your bedroom, prop up a pillow. Pretend that the pillow is the person that hurt you. Tell the pillow (person) what they did that hurt you. Repeat this process again. Now repeat it again. Start and stop three separate times telling this pillow (person) what they did that hurt you. You may want to punch the pillow as a cathartic release of emotions.

Mental Action:

Repeat these affirmations morning and night:

Scars are evidence of God's love for me because I remember that He saved me.
My God saved me.
I am engraved on His hands.

For the full list of affirmations, go to
https://beckyjonesbtcoach.com/freeactionguide

EMOTIONS IN BETRAYAL TRAUMA

I n this chapter, we'll talk about some difficult emotions that come with betrayal trauma. Pain, anger, fear, triggers, and trauma are all difficult emotions you'll feel on your journey. Of course, these aren't all the emotions you'll feel, but these are emotions I want to address.

Pain

The pain of betrayal trauma is more than a discomfort or irritation. It's pure agony. It burns and blazes inside. It's a burning fire that won't be thrown off. You feel like it's melting you on the inside. It's also heavy and suffocating. The heaviness of the pain makes it hard to breathe. I would have to tell myself to breathe. Topping it off like a choke cherry on top of an ice cream sundae, there was no relief.

And there it stays.

It's hard to breathe. It's hard to function. It's hard to think. I couldn't eat and lost weight. If you've ever experienced the death of a loved one, it's a very similar feeling. The grief buries you alive.

When I first found out about the betrayal, I sat in burning pain. I hurt past anything I thought was possible to feel and still live. I was crying multiple times a day. I couldn't think. So many emotions were running through me at lightning speed. And I had no relief.

So much of the pain was from the deception. Everything that I thought was real and true wasn't anymore. What I thought was ground wasn't, so it was difficult to get my bearings. This added to the pain because my world was spinning. I didn't know what was real anymore.

Every part of my life was affected by pain: my brain, my sleeping, my eating, my social, emotional, and mental capacity. The pain shut me down in every facet of my life.

I was in a daze and could barely function. I couldn't think. And I'm not just saying that. I literally couldn't think. I had a haziness in my head that I couldn't push past. My kids would ask me simple questions and I would just stare at them because I didn't understand the words coming out of their mouth. Unless items were written down, I couldn't remember what I needed to buy at the grocery store. I couldn't grasp any sense of a schedule, and couldn't remember where anyone was supposed to be.

During this time, my kids noticed and picked up the slack. They would make decisions on their own when I didn't know the answer. They would come with me to the store and decide what they wanted to eat and get the ingredients. I was so grateful for that.

I couldn't push past this. I didn't know what was happening to my mind.

I lost my appetite and struggled to eat. I lost weight. I didn't know what was happening to my body. It was actually <u>hard</u> to eat, and I had to force myself to eat something.

I was grateful when night came, but it was hard to sleep. And if I did fall asleep, I would easily wake up. The pain was always there. As soon as I woke up, I would feel it. It was absolutely awful. I found no relief.

A lot of the pain was in loneliness. Socially, I immediately withdrew from everyone. I stopped running with friends. I stopped talking to friends. When I did open up to someone, I dealt with the fear that they too would betray me. I slowly pulled away from everyone. And many friends and family members did betray me as they wrestled with their own pain of the situation. No one was safe. I didn't trust anyone to process on. Some people whom I tried to process on, didn't handle it well, and that made it so much worse. In my situation, no one was safe because they were all reeling from the shock of the situation

I felt mental pain. People looked at me differently. Since something like this happened to me, then something must have been wrong with ME. Shame is real. Shame comes not only outwardly but also inwardly. Then, you look around at your friends and wonder why it happened to you. It adds to the inner dialogue you have looping in your head that there's something wrong with you. That inner looping in my head caused a great deal of mental pain. I had never known mental pain before, but it's real, and it's exhausting.

I was so grateful for anyone who did anything to try to ease my pain. I would numbly accept it. When people said they were willing to help and asked what I needed, I didn't know. I honestly couldn't think. I was grateful for those people who just saw a need and filled it.

I was overwhelmed at the path ahead of me. It looked long and suffocating and hopeless. My life had been completely blown apart, and I didn't know where to start putting it back together again.

Anger

Anger is a huge, ugly and heavy feeling. I felt angry for other people's choices that hurt me. I feel anger not only for that but also for their blaming me for their choices and even their anger toward me. I felt angry about how I was being treated.

Anger is a scary beast. It scares me to feel anger because I'm afraid it will overtake me. When I feel anger, I can see why people do crazy things.

I didn't know what to do with anger. I didn't even acknowledge I had anger because I was afraid that if I it did, I couldn't control it. I was afraid it would overtake me and stay.

I thought that keeping anger deeply buried was a good thing. I thought it was bad to feel anger. I would slap my hand any time a hint of it came up. How unrighteous! I wanted to be righteous. I was being a good saint to keep it down there and deny that it even existed.

I thought if I didn't acknowledge the anger, then maybe eventually it would go away. But that's not true. Not acknowledging anger just means that it builds up inside my body and soul like a gelatin dessert and there was nothing sweet about this layered concoction.

My heart and gut knew it was there even though my brain said it wasn't. My body needed it gone. It needed to be free. Truth sets you free. Freedom didn't come from packing it down. Freedom came from working through it.

I would have to face the ugly beast of anger if I was ever to let it go. In therapy, I realized that I had packed anger down so deeply and then protected that anger with layers of sadness. Sadness kept it safely hidden. Sadness was an easier emotion for me to deal with. So, there it was: anger packed deep inside me because I had no idea how to deal with my anger.

Fear

Fear takes away my breath.

I've been ruled by fear most of my life: fear of what will happen and fear of not being loved. I struggled to feel safe.

Then God plopped the biggest fear I ever had in my lap. It was now my reality and not just my imagination. I stood and stared at sexual betrayal. It wasn't just the monster in my closet. It was out and sitting in front of me. It was real. I realized as I kept staring at that big black mass of fear, that I would need to pick it up and figure out how to deal with it. Otherwise it would overtake my life.

Triggers

Triggers are like a big, unexpected wave from the ocean of life that knocks me off my feet. I'll be going along just fine and then out of the blue, a memory or a smell or the sight of someone or the way someone treats me will send my heart-rate skyrocketing and my brain spinning.

One of the hardest things about betrayal trauma is being triggered.

Triggers are so unfair. Triggers are heartless and ruthless. Triggers will take a wonderful moment and, in a matter of seconds, turn it into a bad moment.

In the beginning of my betrayal trauma, I didn't even know what the word "trigger" meant. Everyone in the betrayal trauma field kept using that term. But slowly, I started to define what they were for me. After all, triggers have to be defined and validated and dealt with before I can walk through them and overcome them.

What are triggers? They are sights, smells, flashes of memories, or anything that will send you back to a place of trauma. For example, if you were bitten by a dog when you were younger, every time you see a dog, you break out in a cold sweat, your heart rate starts racing, and you wanted to run away. Triggers are personal and are different for everyone. Like your own personal puzzle, you need to figure out, piece by piece, what sends you into a place of trauma.

Trauma

Betrayal trauma is real. It's the most terrifying feeling of insecurity. It's like I'm in the middle of an open field and I hear gunshots coming from the trees but there's NO cover for me. I'm in the middle of the field and getting shot at and I can do nothing. I'm vulnerable. In that moment, I feel the biggest rush of emotion: panic, fear, anxiety to a degree that blows my brain so that nothing cognitive is left. I have only an animalistic instinct to fight or flee, to *survive*.

Betrayal trauma is real. My day may go along fine and then like an ocean wave out of nowhere, a trigger will hit me and knock me over. Then I'm submerged and dragged out to sea by a riptide of emotions.

I experience betrayal trauma in different ways. I feel a cloak of heaviness come over me. My heart starts to hurt. My heart pounds like I'm in danger. My head becomes super fuzzy. I struggle to think. Sometimes, the world spins and I become disoriented. My stomach starts turning and I can't eat. Like a hungry lion, out of my gut lunges a feeling of panic and then my brain pounds a thought in my head, *Get out, get out! You're not safe! You're not safe!*

One day, while in the grocery store, I saw someone who wasn't safe next to the lettuce. I had a panic attack. But I had to keep it together long enough to tie up the apples and walk past that person. I shamed myself for the trauma I felt.

In this chapter, we talked about some emotions you'll feel when you've been sexually betrayed: pain, anger, fear, triggers, and trauma. In the next chapter, we'll discuss ideas on how to deal with these emotions.

YOUR ACTION PLAN

Journal:

- What emotions are you feeling?

Physical Action:

- Tonight, while you're lying in your bed, closing your eyes, trying to sleep, go back to a scene during the day that brought you fear, anger, or trauma. Pretend you're floating above that scene, watching yourself. Watch what happened in the scene. Slow it down and see what you're feeling, smelling, hearing. Who is in the scene? What are they saying? Watch yourself below you and how you feel with every movement or shift in the scene. See where your heart elevated and your emotions changed. See where you don't feel safe and where your emotions spiraled out of control.
- After you've watched the scene, replay it again in your mind. Is there anything you would change? Is there anything you could do to help you bring back power into that moment for you? For me, sometimes, it was as simple as straightening out my back and standing up taller to bring confidence back into myself.

Mental Action:

Repeat these affirmations morning and night:

My emotions are teaching me information about myself. Listen.
I can take care of my needs.

For the full list of affirmations, go to
https://beckyjonesbtcoach.com/freeactionguide

IDEAS ON HOW TO MOVE THROUGH PAIN, ANGER, FEAR, TRIGGERS AND TRAUMA

Dealing with difficult emotions has been one of the greatest rocks I've picked up on my journey through betrayal trauma. I've grown in my ability to take care of myself emotionally. I've learned so much about feelings: what they are and how to deal with them. I'll share with you this pebble I've put in my pocket.

A problem of betrayal trauma is that I feel an emotion faster than I know *why* I'm feeling it. If I don't slow down, the emotions will leak out and cause damage.

I've never been good at slow.

When the worse thing I could imagine happened, it broke me into a thousand pieces. God then began His work to put me back together in a healthy, strong, and whole way. He took all those pieces and started rebuilding me piece by piece. A huge part of putting me back together in a strong and whole way was emotional management and learning how to deal with hard feelings.

"Real power comes from knowing we can take care of ourselves, even when we feel emotional pain. However, emotional pain does not have to devastate us. We can sit still, feel the pain, figure out if there's something

- 33 -

we need to do to take care of ourselves and then go on with our life. While hurt feelings aren't as much fun as feeling happy, they are, still, just feelings. We can surrender to them, feel them, and go on."[11]

The dishes clanked as I numbly rinsed the soapy dishes under the running warm water and put them in the dishwasher. Through the clanking, I listened to a podcast in which a lady talked about how she struggled underneath the crushing weight of the feelings she experienced with her little daughter dying. Even though we had different experiences, she was describing the crushing weight I felt. I was intrigued.

She said mindfulness helped her.[12]

What is mindfulness? I finished up the dishes, dried my hands and sat at the computer and typed in mindfulness on Google.

"Mindfulness - a mental state achieved by focusing one's awareness on the present moment, while calmly acknowledging and accepting one's feelings, thoughts, and bodily sensations, used as a therapeutic technique.[13]

Another website [14]explained that practicing mindfulness looked like breathing in and out slowly and focusing on my breath. I was also supposed to empty my brain of thoughts.

What was this simple task supposed to accomplish? How could this help me deal with my heavy emotions?

I have to admit that I was very skeptical at how this process could help this lady deal with her painful feelings of her young daughter passing. But I persisted doing it because she testified of how much it helped her.

I took my kids to Riggins, Idaho so that they could find garnets. The place was next to a wide, rushing river. As they looked for garnets, I sat on

[11] Beattie, Melody. *Language of Letting Go*. Page 7-8. Place of publication not identified: Hay House Inc, 2005.
[12] "Seeing Green: Jill Thomas." Seeing Green | Jill Thomas | Inspiration. Accessed February 8, 2020. https://www.churchofjesuschrist.org/inspiration/latter-day-saints-channel/watch/series/hope-works/seeing-green-jill-thomas-hope-works?lang=eng.
[13] "Mindfulness." Dictionary.com. Dictionary.com. Accessed February 8, 2020. https://www.dictionary.com/browse/mindfulness.
[14] Bayes-Fleming, Nicole, Grace Bullock, Barry Boyce, Crystal Goh, Kira M. Newman, and Linda Graham. "Getting Started with Mindfulness." Mindful, September 14, 2018. https://www.mindful.org/meditation/mindfulness-getting-started/.

a large rock, watching this wide river of beautiful blue water rush by. When I'm practicing mindfulness, I like to imagine myself on that rock next to the river. The river is my feelings. Occasionally I see a huge ripple rush up or I see small waves gently foaming around the shore. I see these as my feelings and I'm just watching them.

When I first started doing mindfulness, I thought there was no way I could look at my feelings as something disconnected from me and NOT me. It was very discouraging. But the more I watched my feelings come and go, the better I got at it. It was like a muscle that grew stronger inside of me. Honestly, my ability to look at my emotions like that gives me a lot of freedom.

One of the benefits of mindfulness is that it teaches me to disconnect myself from my feelings. I'm not my feelings. Emotions come and go upon me but those feelings are not who I am. When I see emotions in that way, I'm better able to go back and see where my emotion came from and validate why I'm feeling that. Then I'm not judging or shaming myself but taking care of myself while I'm feeling and sitting in that emotion and either work to let it go or wait for it to pass. And through this process, I remember my supreme value and worth despite what I'm feeling.

My feelings tell me something. Sometimes, my feelings tell me that injustice has happened and it's not right. Sometimes, my feelings tell me that I'm angry at another for what they did to me. Sometimes my feelings tell me that I'm sad. I listen to my feelings and what those feelings are telling me. These feelings give me insight about myself. They help me create connections about myself and my world and who I am and what I need. These insights are precious. Once those insights are gained, then the feeling sometimes goes away or is less intense. Those feelings finally did their job and told me what I needed to learn.

I've learned to be kind to myself in my feelings. Being kind to myself looks like me not getting upset with myself that I feel angry. It looks like me not shaming myself for my feelings.

I've learned to validate myself. Validation looks like me acknowledging that there was a reason why I felt that way. That validation allows me not to stuff down my feelings. The truth of why I feel the way I do often sets me free.

When feelings sometimes sit on me and won't release, I have to practice a lot of self-care until they let go. Sometimes, I know why I'm feeling a certain way, but I still can't get past it. At those times, I do everything I can to work through the steps to take care of myself, acknowledge and validate, rinse and repeat, until they let go.

As you work to recover from betrayal trauma, you gain tools to deal with whatever emotions come up. Safety comes from knowing you have the tools to deal with whatever emotions come up.

Mindfulness and Breathing

First, I breathe in and out. I close my eyes and focus on my breathing. When the body feels a fear, we shorten our breath and breathe faster. Our body goes into fight or flight. My daughter told me that studies show that when you're stressed, you stop breathing, so if you choose to get your body breathing again, then you can decrease your heartbeat and your reaction.

As I choose to control my physical body and deepen my breath, my brain starts to slow down and not just react. My brain thinks it's safe because I'm choosing to calm it. This takes a lot of practice. The more I did mindfulness, the better I became at calming myself and grounding myself. Breathing began to be the beginning of the new ground I would stand on. Breathing would form the building blocks of a new security found only in myself and in my God.

As I breathe, I focus on the present moment. At first, this was so hard for me. My mind was racing and I couldn't stay focused very long. But I got better at it. And it definitely helped me.

If I have time, I do guided meditations with mindfulness. Sometimes, when I go to a place of fear, my thoughts go wild and I think about things that aren't necessarily true. It's important to fill my mind with truth when I feel afraid. Guided meditations put truth back into my mind. I can cling to that truth instead of dwelling on things that I think are true but aren't.

When I've calmed down enough, I try to see where the emotion came up. As I walked back through what happened, I found the moment where the emotion came upon me. I can validate myself and say, "Yes, that would be a difficult place. I can see why it came." This allows a space and moment to validate myself. That validation feels good. The feeling that came is real. What I'm feeling is real. The pain is real. The anger is real. The emotion is real. I validate, validate, validate. I don't stuff it down. It's true; I do feel that way and there's a reason why.

Validation

One of the difficulties of betrayal trauma for me was that for a long time, outside sources told me my feelings were silly and unfounded. Even when I found out that everything I felt WAS true and real, I still had to relearn not to shame myself in my own emotions. Because I had been treated that way by others for so long, it was difficult to do. I had to learn to stop shaming myself.

If my body is telling me it's afraid by a sudden increased heart rate, and I keep telling myself that it's dumb and shove the fear down inside me, the fear won't go away but will continue. I'm ignoring a natural defense mechanism in myself.

If I'm feeling angry, it's telling me a boundary of mine was violated. If I ignore how I feel, I lose valuable information about what my body is telling me.

Others let me down by not validating how I felt but I won't do that to myself. I won't ever again shame the emotions that I feel.

Facing the Emotion

If I'm validating myself, then I'll need to face the emotion and be curious about why it came up. Maybe it wasn't something that happened but a memory that came up that caused emotion. I face that memory. Facing it looks like writing about that memory or reliving it in my mind. This is another deeper way to validate how I feel. I remember or write about it again from all the senses: what it smelled like, what the colors were in the scene, what the different feelings were, how others were behaving. I write about it all. Sometimes, a memory and the accompanying emotion might keep coming up. So I might have to write about it multiple times. The important thing is to not stuff my emotion or memory. I need to keep the emotion flowing like a healthy stream of water, not a stagnant, smelly pond that just sits inside me. Also, if it's too hard to do that on my own, I'll need a therapist to help me.

Writing

Writing is the safest place for me to get out how I feel. A blank piece of paper has no bias, no restrictions on what I can't or can say, and it's open and inviting. That blank piece of paper doesn't care if I write splotchy and sporadic words dampened with big, wet tear drops. The paper doesn't care if I make any sense at all. It doesn't care if my sentences are spoken in correct English or even if my words are misspelled. It accepts me as me.

After writing down how I feel, I wriggle my hand past all the yucky leftover kitchen garbage to throw the paper away in the bottom of the kitchen garbage can, far down enough that no one would see or wonder what that paper contained. When I had access to a wood stove, I tossed it in the stove and burned it. Either way, it's so satisfying to pour out my feelings and get rid of it in a burning heap or under scraps of kitchen food.

Writing is especially helpful for me when I deal with anger. Dr. Skinner says that we "access rage and the story behind it by journaling."[15]

According to Melody Beattie, "Anger is a powerful and sometimes frightening emotion. It's also a beneficial one if it's not allowed to harden into resentment or used as a battering ram to punish or abuse people. Anger is a warning signal. It points to problems. Sometimes it's prob-

---

15 How Do I Manage My Anger & Rage? "How Do I Manage My Anger & Rage?" Bloom For Women, November 17, 2017. https://bloomforwomen.com/how-do-i-manage-my-anger-rage/.

lems we need to solve. Sometimes it points to boundaries we need to set. Sometimes, it's the final burst of energy before letting go, or acceptance, settles in. *I will feel and release any angry feelings I have today. I can do that appropriately and safely."*[16]

After writing about it, I ask myself what I believed because of that memory. My emotions: pain, anger, and fear sometimes stem from what I believe about myself because of how someone else treated me. I might believe that I should have known what was happening. I might believe it was because I wasn't enough. Are those statements really true? My work is revealed when I see the tight knot of lies I believed and need to unravel. If I can stop believing those lies, peace and resolution can be found.

In writing it out, I might see that my anger, sadness, grief, or pain was there to protect me from the hurt, neglect, or abandonment I feel. My work is revealed when I see the underlying issues that need to be resolved before the emotion can go away.

Clearing out lies and seeing my emotions for what they are clears the path for me to see truth. The truth in sexual betrayal is that their behavior has nothing to do with me.

One truth I'll share with you is that my anger was there to protect me from the abandonment that I felt. However, I can choose to work through my abandonment feelings. Then comes a beautiful place where I can forgive myself for believing the lies and reacting and, thus, clear the way to forgive them for believing lies too.

Acceptance is huge in working through anger, pain, grief, and triggers. As I write about what really happened, it helps me see truth. Accepting and acknowledging helps me move on with reality. I accept what someone did to me with true understanding of lessons learned and not with sugar-coated platitudes and I move on from there.

---

[16] Beattie, Melody. *Language of Letting Go.* Page 59. Place of publication not identified: Hay House Inc, 2005.

Emotional Regulation in the Heat of the Moment

How do I deal with emotions when I'm facing them at the moment? First, I think this just takes a lifetime of practice. I have to choose to be still. If I'm staring anger in the face, I start by breathing. I also get myself out of the situation. I know I'll burn hot, so I don't even mess with my weaknesses. I get out. I can't deal with it at the moment. It's kind of like a shark, once those eyes roll back, there's no stopping its fierce jaw from clamping down with a huge force of pressure. This is me when anger or other hard emotion comes. I have to cool off before I incinerate. So, first, space is key for me.

Another part of this emotion principle is that if I act out in emotion, the person is most likely to hear the anger and not my true pain. I don't want to act out because then the focus will be on my misbehavior not their misbehavior. And to be honest, I don't think that people even care to hear how you feel at the moment. They're most likely in survival mode too.

Fight, flight, or freeze modes come when we don't feel safe. I don't let my feelings escalate to fight mode. It only hurts me. Yes, I'm justified to be angry, but if I fight back with anger, it will only hurt me. I fight back in different ways using clear language and working hard to disconnect from their crazy making. I can stand in my truth, which is how I feel, and let it stay there. They won't fix it or change, but I can at least say my thoughts in a rational way.

I'm better able to "fight" this way as I prepare for "battle" by working out my anger beforehand and envisioning myself staying calm. If a topic light me up, I do intense work on my side to figure out why I have so much emotion there. Then when I go back into the arena of discourse, I'm better able to leave anger at the door so that the conversation can be focused and kept on my pain and the actions that are causing the pain.

Talking

Having safe people to talk too is super important, people who wouldn't judge me in my ugly hour. Honestly, I was afraid to open up to people, but when God told me it was okay to open up and I did, it yielded wonderful healing connections and advice for me. I found that I always knew when I needed to talk to someone and I always knew who. So, I relied on that inner voice to tell me it was okay to speak and open up.

I've been blessed to know who my friends were and who had my back. I knew who I should call, and they knew just what to say. I loved their thoughts, even the ones that were hard to hear. I love my friends for their honesty and perspective. They've been a wonderful and safe place. Those wonderful friends validated me, listened to me, and calmed me. They reassured me of my value and they helped me discern what was my stuff and what wasn't.

Crying

I cry. Crying gets out my emotions. It seems like its nature's way to get out what's on the inside of us. Sometimes, when the pain gets so bad, I sob and cry so hard that my shoulders ache afterwards.

I give myself space to be messy with my emotions. I cry in the woods where no one can see me. I cry in my closet where hopefully no one can hear me. I cry in my car. I cry in the therapist's office. I cry with safe people.

My hard cries can be ugly, so it's good to have a space to be authentic and pour out my ugly emotions.

Exercise

Exercise is a huge way for me to manage my emotions. I exercise because I need to physically release the feelings I have inside of me. I need to move. Sometimes, I walk. Sometimes, I run. I try to exercise outside. It's critical for me to get outside so that the pain that's so huge inside me, can spill out into the outdoors. Even if the weather is bad, I go. Somehow, if it's raining and windy, going outside in that weather helped purge out the yuck I felt as I overcame the weather enough to exercise. It gave me confidence. Also, eating healthy, eating lots of leafy greens, and not eating sugar helps a ton.

Prayer

I pray. Always, I pray to my God, my Higher Power. I pray a lot. Prayer brings huge amounts of relief as I soak my pillow with tears multiple times a day. I pray both vocally and silently. When I want to talk out loud, I pray in my closet.

If I'm around other people, I pray in my mind.

I pray for help. I pray to know how to take care of myself. I pray for relief from pain. I pray to feel hope. I pray to feel peace. I pray to take away the shame I feel and to feel good about myself. I pray for love for myself and for others. I pray for strength. I pray to know that God is there. I pray to know that God is just.

Help from your God is available. The gifts only He can give are available. He knows everything. He knows what you need. Pray always.

I'm praying all the time inside my mind and heart or kneeling down when no one is looking. I know God is always there. Every time I cry out for help, God helps me. He brings peace and reassurance that He is there. I'm never left alone.

I just described how I deal with emotions when they hit me and how I work to get those unpleasant emotions out of my system. Much like a water bottle full of dirty water, I need to empty it before I can put good water in. Here is how I put good water in me:

Imagery

I try a lot of things at home with myself to retrain my brain. If I see that a situation keeps coming up and causes my heart to start racing, I'll do my own imagery work. That looks like me lying down on the bed or sitting in a chair in a quiet environment and closing my eyes and imagining myself going through that situation. I pretend I'm watching myself go through it, much like a movie. That's important because it helps me see where the fear, triggers, pain, or anger come from. I also see myself have success in that situation. It's often fun to write the script of how I want the situation to turn out. It's a simple thing to do and very helpful for me. I've overcome many places of fear using this method.

Imagery is huge in emotional management. Reactive people are difficult to communicate with. Imagery takes me out of the emotion and helps me look at it objectively. It helps me see it like a movie and that objectivity will grow stronger and I become less and less reactive. This practice actually rewires your brain so that you no longer react habitually to negative situations.

Reading

I read. I read anything I can get my hands on about betrayal trauma.

I joined bloomforwomen.com, a website devoted to helping women heal from betrayal trauma. SO much information is on this website. The information I learned about betrayal trauma helped me understand the new world I was living in.

Much like aloe on a sunburn, reading about betrayal trauma provided so much relief from the pain I felt. I read about managing my emotions. I read stories about how people handled their trauma. It gave me ideas. It helped me understand what I was feeling. I didn't feel crazy anymore. Any topic that I felt my soul hungered to know more about, I would read. Reading helps me not feel alone or weird. Reading helped me feel normal in my responses to betrayal trauma. I felt hope because I read about tools that could help me.

I read the Scriptures. I would read them in the morning, afternoon, and evening. I was reading all the time. When I read, I was searching for answers to my questions: how do I act, how do I respond, how do I keep a bigger perspective, how do I forgive, how do I love, how do I heal?

Reading helped my pain because I gained knowledge and a bigger perspective through reading and studying the Word of God. I'm a firm believer that God will speak to you. He spoke to me when I read. I was daily pounding on the doors of Heaven. Although, I wasn't given all the knowledge at once, I would read, and peace would come. I would read, and a snippet of understanding and knowledge would come. I would read, and perspective would come.

Affirmations

Saying affirmations is another way I pour good, clean water into my soul. Affirmations are positive statements of belief. They are called power statements. They are an instant shot of peace and hope. Affirmations gave me ground to stand on in a shaky world. These were statements that I made for myself and evolved over time as I saw what I needed. I read my affirmations morning and evening. These really help me in my pain and regulating my emotions. Like putting buttery cream over a scraped up knee softens it and relieve pain, just by saying the affirmations, I felt better. I include affirmations at the end of each chapter. You can download all the affirmations and action plan here: https://beckyjonesbtcoach.com/freeactionguide

Outside Help

I had wonderful professionals[17][18]who gave me strategies to work through my anger, pain, triggers, and grief. They helped me face the difficult emotion of anger and work through it. They helped me face the shame I felt. They helped me see what work was mine and what was not. They helped me work to disconnect from lies I had believed about myself because of someone else's behavior. It was so beneficial for me to have professional help.

Doing all these things really helped manage my emotions.

Sometimes, though, the emotions would just sit there and burn. At those moments, when I had done all I could to take care of myself but the

---

[17] "Summers, Melinda." LIFEstory Transformation. Accessed February 8, 2020. http://www.lifestorytransformation.com/summers-melinda.html.

[18] "Eric Mikkelsen - Central Idaho Counseling 125 Commerce St Mccall, ID Marriage & Family Counselors." MapQuest. Accessed February 8, 2020. https://www.mapquest.com/us/idaho/eric-mikkelsen-central-idaho-counseling-351186811.

emotion still burned, I stopped fighting it and accepted it. I sat in it and let it burn. I looked up to God and said, "Okay, if this cup or pain isn't meant to pass, then okay." And I would bow to it.

Learning to sit well in emotions is a good thing to be able to do. People who don't sit well in pain make mistakes that worsen their lives. They go out and spend money. They hurt someone else. They do their own type of betrayal back to their spouse. The better you can manage your emotions, the better you're able to not make mistakes that will harm your life or others' lives. Also, if you sit in pain well, you're better able to become your best self.

Being proactive in my emotions helps my self-esteem so much. Being proactive looks like me taking responsibility for my emotions. When I do this, I feel more in control when my life is out of control. I own my right to choose. I'm a sovereign being with the power of choice for my own life. Knowing that, I'm in a better position to choose what will be healthy for me and not harmful.

I'm responsible for the work I need to do. I'll reap the rewards or consequences of my choices.

As I do my work, I'm blessed with peace and rest and the ability to be my true self.

Emotional management is something I'm always working on. Much like taking out the trash, it needs to be done so that it doesn't build up and block flow within myself. Like a squirrelly cat, I feel like I don't ever have emotional management completely in the bag. Emotional management doesn't mean that I stuff my emotions down inside me, pretend I don't feel them, and be a robot. Emotional management means that I have confidence in my ability to take responsibility for my emotions, face and move through those emotions, and take care of myself when I feel them.

Like a running nose reveals a cold, your emotions can be a symptom of something else. My emotions give me information. So, if I do feel something, I use that to teach me. What is underneath all those feelings? If I can figure it out, then I can more easily let it go or open it up to heal. And when I figure it out, it's a beautiful moment where deep understanding comes. I can forgive myself, love myself, and show compassion for myself. When that happens, I'm better able to give that same love and compassion toward others. My life will always be a process of understanding myself and my experience.

In this chapter, we talked about ideas on how to deal with difficult emotions. Emotional management has blessed my life so much. I count it as one of the huge blessings that came because of sexual betrayal. I'm not perfect at it, but I'm no longer afraid of my emotions or how to deal with them. I can face them and move through them. In the next chapter, we'll talk about how to block out other people's opinions.

YOUR ACTION PLAN

Journal:

- What emotions are you feeling?

Physical Action:

- Do one of the suggestions in this chapter to manage your difficult emotions.

Mental Action:

Repeat this affirmation morning and night:

I can take care of myself emotionally

For the full list of affirmations, go to
https://beckyjonesbtcoach.com/freeactionguide

BLOCKING OUT OTHER PEOPLE'S OPINIONS

I was almost done writing my first book, a memoir called *A Little Tent in the Woods*.[19] This book is about how my husband and I and our five children homesteaded a piece of land and lived in a tent while we built our house. While writing the book, I came to a part where a friend offered services to me one afternoon by letting me use her washing machine and feeding my kids and me a lovely lunch. In the middle of typing and reminiscing about her kindness to me, I picked up my phone to text her. I sent her a message of thanks.

Then, assuming she had caught wind of the sexual betrayal that happened to me, I made a fishing, ripping on myself "joke" intended to reel in a validating statement of my worth and value. "There was probably a reason why this betrayal happened to me." I said to her. My self-incriminating "joke/text" hung in the air like a balloon. I reeled in nothing but silence.

Finally, she texted and asked if I would like to talk to her on the phone. I texted back "sure." She called and after a half an hour of her talking about her life and about how because she was doing all the right things, her life was being blessed. I stopped her and asked about why she didn't respond to my statement and that I needed some validation.

---

[19] Amazon. Accessed February 8, 2020. https://www.amazon.com/Becky-Jones/e/B0779R8QQH/ref=dp_byline_cont_ebooks_1.

I didn't expect her answer.

"You were a very hard wife."

Even as I type this, I'm amazed that she or anyone for that matter could say that. How could she know what type of wife I was? How could she know if I was difficult? The comment stung deeper as I remembered how many times my husband had been gone helping her and her marriage as a religious counselor.

The dagger that was stabbed in my heart by her, twisted back and forth as I realized that, like the story of the Jew in the Bible[20] that was beaten and left for dead, I was passed by and judged unworthy of another's compassion, help, and love. I was judged that it was clearly my fault that someone had beaten me up and left me for dead.

People have so much power in their hands to comfort, sustain, and lift another or to crush them. When people are vulnerable, it's amazing to me the pride and callousness that people have when they see a bullet hole in someone's chest and then push their fingers deeper into the wound and watch them scream in pain. This lady would outwardly proclaim her Christianity to the world, yet here she was on the open road, with no one around to see, kicking the person lying in the dirt and saying it was their fault. I couldn't believe they were so clueless. People are hateful, mean, and full of so much pride. My naive bubble was popped: there was so much evil, pride and spitefulness in the world.

That was the beginning of the end for me. I was done caring about what people thought of me.

But, this wasn't the only time this happened. Immediate family members close to the situation added their judgment.

"Your husband wouldn't have done this, if it hadn't been for you."

---

[20] "Luke 10." The Church of Jesus Christ of Latter-day Saints. Accessed February 8, 2020. https://www.churchofjesuschrist.org/study/scriptures/nt/luke/10.33?lang=eng&clang=eng#p32.

"Maybe now you'll learn to give your husband more space."

"My friend just lost her best friend." (Someone speaking about the mistress "losing" my husband now that the affair was out.)

I had a betrayal trauma coaching client whose spouse was heavily involved in prostitution using human trafficking. When I told them to prepare for backlash once the divorce was made public, they pushed back at me that there was no way that would happen. "It is clearly their issue," they said. But, predictably, it did come. People somehow blamed them for the actions of another.

"You'll be in this place," I assured them. "If not yet, it will come." At this stage, I want you to know it's coming and how to protect yourself from it.

The problem with betrayal is that other's *outside* of the situation will have their opinion.

Blocking out other people's opinions can be a very difficult and hard pebble to pick up, but it's so very valuable. This is a pebble I have to continually put into my pocket. When I think I have this lesson mastered, life throws something else at me and I must once again work on this.

People will have stories about you in their head. To have peace for myself, I cannot own their stories. By not owning them, I mean that I don't need to believe them. I don't need to agree with their perspective. I can believe and know my own story. People slap judgments on what they don't fully understand. People slap judgments to try to control and manipulate. People slap judgments so that they can justify what they want to justify.

Those who betray us will spin a story in their head. They will say that there were reasons why they sexually betrayed you.

I don't need to believe their story. I can be confident in what I know to be true. Even if someone criticizes and shames me for not believing them, I don't need to give into their shame weapon and believe their story. I know of someone who regularly criticized someone's need to find out the truth for themselves and shamed them for not just believing them. They shamed their process of wanting to come to a conclusion on their own and feel good about it in their hearts. Looking back, it was easy for that criticized person to feel shame, "I should be better and just trust you. If I was better, I would just believe you." Someone who really loves you and isn't trying to hide something, embraces the fact that you want to search and discover and know for yourself. It strengthens you as an individual and as a partner in a marriage. Being critical or shaming is a warning flag that the story is all about them to begin with and has no space for you anyway.

People who didn't know me well and learned of the sexual betrayal that came upon me drew their own conclusions. They made up a story that their mind could wrap around. Sometimes, that story is favorable toward me. Sometimes, it's not. One thing that was surprising to me was the judgement that was passed upon me. I definitely didn't see that coming. It's very difficult when people judge you because of what happened to you.

I realized that if they could put a story or label around it, then they could try to control it happening to them.

Elizabeth Smart, the girl who was made famous because she was abducted out her bedroom window, wrote an Instagram post that says it perfectly.

> The last few days I've been reminded of something that took me awhile to learn after I was rescued. It is so easy to focus on all the negative things that happen and to feel that everything is unfair and should not have happened to you. Well I think you're right. Too many things happen that you don't deserve, and are unfair. But even though bad things happen they often lead to knowledge, compassion, understanding, empathy, love, healing, and change. In my book all those things are good. Out of great darkness light often shines through. I see that in my own life. Perhaps the only way for me to be where I am today was by going through

everything that I did. I never asked to be kidnapped, and nor would I ever want it to happen again to me or anyone else. <u>But had I not been kidnapped and raped, I wouldn't understand what it is to be a victim/ survivor</u>, *<u>I would naively think that the victims would have some responsibility over what happened to them, I would have built barriers between what happened to them and what could never happen to me. There would be so much I wouldn't know or understand.</u>* Looking back, I can honestly say it was the worst experience I have ever dealt with and I hope no one ever goes through it again but I am also grateful it happened to me for what it has taught me and allowed me to be a part of, and for making me into the person I am today.[21]

I think if sexual betrayal had not happened to me, I could have easily been one of those people who judge the betrayed spouse or partner and thought that they could have done something to prevent it: cooked better food, been thinner, kept a better house, been less emotional, or whatever. If those are the glasses they look through, then it's easy to control the situation. Then, it's just a matter of what you should do or not do. If I keep a clean house, unlike this person who got betrayed, then my spouse won't look elsewhere. If I'm skinny, unlike this person, then my spouse will be faithful. It's a beautiful framework to give you the illusion that you have some control and can prevent it from happening to you. After all, I'm not like them; I'm a great spouse, so sexual betrayal won't happen to me.

It's such a false foundation, yet it's done every day in the minds of so many.

When someone betrays you sexually, that's a sign that something bigger is amiss than the house being unkept or being able to cook a good meal.

[21] "Elizabeth Smart (@elizabeth_smart_official) • Instagram Photos and Videos." Instagram. Accessed February 8, 2020. Post on June 20,2018. https://www.instagram.com/elizabeth_smart_official/?hl=en.

Sexual betrayal, at a core level involves poor coping habits with any kind of emotion. It also involves connection issues. When you have poor coping habits and connection issues, it's difficult to maintain and sustain a healthy, committed, long-term relationship.

It's not about you. I don't care what people tell you. Don't believe it. They can have their opinions. It doesn't mean they're true.

I don't need to own someone else's story. They have no idea. Their stories and ideas cause me pain. Eventually, like a hot potato in my hand, I had to let them go and believe in what I know. I let go of those stories by being confident in what I know and believe. I trust myself and I don't need validation from others to sustain that trust.

But, trust in myself was damaged. Ultimately that's why I was vulnerable to what someone else said and their story. But I worked on trusting myself and believing that I do know the truth. I believe that God gave me truth for myself.

"And awake, and arise from the dust, O Jerusalem; yea, and put on thy beautiful garments, O daughter of Zion; and strengthen thy stakes and enlarge thy borders forever, that thou mayest no more be confounded, that the covenants of the Eternal Father which he hath made unto thee, O house of Israel, may be fulfilled."[22]

Strengthen who you are. Know who you are regardless of the stories that are swirling around you. Just because someone says or believes something different than you, it doesn't mean it's true. Be confident of the truth that you have within yourself that guides you.

I cannot control the stories that other people have in their head. But I can control the stories that I have in my head.

Here's what I do:

- **Recognize the reality that people's opinions may not change, and that's okay.** I dip my big toe in the water and see if they're

---

[22] "Moroni 10:31." The Church of Jesus Christ of Latter-day Saints. Accessed February 8, 2020. https://www.churchofjesuschrist.org/study/scriptures/bofm/moro/10.4-5?lang=eng.

open to my truth. If they're not, it's difficult and deadly to try to convince them otherwise. I've tried that before and it just got messy, personal, and mean. Then they feel the need to plaster on the wall ANY mistake they saw me make as a spouse. It's horrible.

Very few of us can see into the heart of another person unless it's given to us by God. We struggle with compassion. We struggle with empathy. We choose to block ourselves from the privilege to see another as God sees us because then WE would have to change. It's easier not to change ourselves but to pound into the other person that they need to change.

1. If I find myself in this place, I say my truth and walk away. I also accept that others hearing my truth may not change their opinions.
2. If I'm sitting in the pain of it, I breathe and take care of myself while I feel the pain.
3. I process it by writing out my anger.
4. I process it by talking to a friend who's safe.
5. I don't lash out at the other person for their opinion. Luckily, I was smart enough in my pain to not lash out at others, but it was SO difficult to bear. Because of how difficult it was for me to bear the pain of other people's opinions, I have and will make the choice to walk away from that person or relationship and never enter it again. I let go of the relationship to sustain myself.

Those who take advantage of us, kick us when we're down, or slap judgments on us so they don't have to be civilized and kind to us aren't safe people.

- **Look around you; many amazing people thrive despite others not seeing them for who they really are.** One of the ideas that brought me great comfort was that so many couldn't see Jesus

Christ for what He was. Many called Him the devil, many didn't understand His words. Christ was able to block out other people's opinions. How did He do it? Truth of who *He* was, His divinity, was powerful inside of Him. How? Because He connected through prayer *so* often with His Higher Power, His God, His Father. The strength to sustain that perspective of who He was came from that connection. Likewise, when I'm connected to my Higher Power and my God, I'm able to withstand other people's untrue and hurtful opinions.

- **Ask why it's hurting?** I ask myself why I really care. Usually it's because I believe there may be an element of truth. Is there something I need to repent of? Do I have unfinished business inside of myself? If I don't believe it's true inside myself, it shows me I have work to do inside my heart and mind to believe in my own goodness and value. Also, if I'm working as hard as I can to keep God's commandments and be worthy of His spirit, then there's one voice of correction or opinion I need to hearken to. Similarly, if someone else says something, and the spirit testifies its true, I'll listen to it.

- **Lose your pride.** I shed several pounds when I experienced betrayal trauma. But I also shed my pride. I *had* to let my pride go to survive. I *had* to stop caring what people think. Pride is putting the opinions of man before God. Whenever I start to go down that road of caring what someone thinks I remind myself that it's pride, and I check myself. "Don't care about what anyone but God thinks, Becky," I tell myself.

- **Let go of the need for validation from others and find it in yourself.** We'll discuss this in the next chapter.

You'll encounter people having hurtful opinions on your road to healing from betrayal trauma. When this happens, recognize the reality that people's opinions may not change, and that's okay. I recognize that amazing people who thrive despite others not seeing them for who they really are. I ask myself why it's hurting. I lose my pride. I also let go of my need for validation.

In this chapter we talked about ways we can block out other people's opinions. In the next chapter, we'll talk about letting go of the need for validation and finding it in yourself.

YOUR ACTION PLAN

Journal:

- How are you feeling hurt by other people's opinions? Get it out of your body and mind by journaling about it.
- What person do you admire who handles other people's adverse opinions well?

Physical Action:

- Lie down and visualize a scene where someone is telling you their hurtful opinion. Visualize how you would handle yourself in that situation, both what you would call handling it appropriately and not appropriately.
- I want you to visualize a hot potato in your hand. It hurts you while you hold it. Why is it hurting you? Look deep in your soul and tell me why their opinion is hurting you.

Mental Action:

Repeat these affirmations morning and night:

I can acknowledge the pain but choose to act like Jesus Christ.
I can let go of what is hurting me.

For the full list of affirmations, go to
https://beckyjonesbtcoach.com/freeactionguide

BREAKING THE CHAINS. LETTING GO OF THE NEED FOR VALIDATION FROM OTHERS AND FINDING IT IN YOURSELF.

Validation is very important but only when it comes from healthy people.

In the betrayal trauma arena, I encountered those that could and should have validated me but they chose not to. I kept going back to a dry well, expecting there to be water. I was left carrying an empty bucket and the most horrifying feeling of abandonment.

The best vignette of how this feels is the story about the research they conducted on abandonment and how it affects children. They put the mother in front of a crying baby and the mother just stared at the baby and didn't pick it up or comfort it. She just stared at the baby. The baby cried worse and worse as the mother just sat there staring at the baby. It was awful watching the video showing the child cry harder and harder.

This was the arena I was living in. Like a child jumping up and down to try to reach a piece of candy from an older sibling, I was jumping up and down trying to get some validation. I could never get it. Soon, cold reactions to my feelings just gas-lighted me. I became emotionally reactive.

I expected a simple understanding. When it wasn't there, I felt like I was going crazy. I really felt like it *was* me. Something was wrong with *me*. I swam in a hot pot of "I'm a horrible person" soup. Sometimes it gets so bad that you wonder why you're even alive since you do the world no good.

I had to break the chains: break the desire I had for validation from the one who betrayed me and seek healthy people and relationships to validate me. Unhealthy people or relationships *don't* validate you.

There's a problem with seeking validation from unhealthy people. Addicts can't validate themselves. That's where sexual betrayal starts. That's why they go to inappropriate sources to validate themselves. They certainly won't be able to validate you. Addicts that can't validate aren't in recovery. This is a dry well. You won't get the validation from this person but only table turning, anger, gas lighting, blame, shame, and lying.

Break the chains. Let go of the need for validation. How do you break the chains?

Notice how I use the word chain as a descriptor for this. I didn't use a string. I didn't use a fishing line. I used a descriptor that describes a strong, iron material that is linked together and used to carry heavy loads. It's not easy to break the need for validation from your unhealthy partner.

The chain was built link by link over time. The first chain linked and forged in our minds around what our concept of marriage should look like. What did your idea of marriage look like? My idea was that marriage was where you love each other and never leave each other even though they drive you nuts and where you work it out and figure it out and don't give up on each other. That's a core belief inside me and how I viewed marriage.

The second link was trust. I trust you. I trust your opinion. I trust your motives. I trust your commitment. My seeking validation from you has always been a core human need since I'm in an intimate relationship with you. It's hard to break the chain of validation when I've used it for so many years.

Another link in the chains of validation could be religiously motivated. One of my links was religiously motivated. If you're a woman and a wife, your husband's opinion was everything, almost like God himself. If I'm standing in that place, then I need my husband's approval and blessing.

Can you start to see why it would be so hard to break your need for validation from your spouse? If you were a dutiful wife that for years hung onto his words, council, and thoughts like they were the law and the will of God, or that he really had your interests at heart, then it's going to be difficult to not keep going back to this and to keep trying to get the validation you need.

It's here in this space you need to discover what framework you're coming from, what the links are in your chain that keep you going back to a dry well to seek his approval or opinion if he just sexually betrayed you.

I had to face my framework in order to break the chains and stop seeking validation from someone who betrayed me. I had to face my personal reasons why I kept going back to a dry well, whether it was because of a habit of trust, the idea of what marriage was supposed to be, or religious tradition.

"Awake, and arise from the dust, O Jerusalem; yea, and put on thy beautiful garments, O daughter of Zion; and strengthen thy stakes and enlarge thy borders forever, that thou mayest no more be confounded."23

It's difficult to do with someone you thought was safe and trusting. Before knowledge of the sexual betrayal came out, I didn't know what I was dealing with. I kept seeking validation from someone I thought was safe and who I didn't know was betraying me. It did a lot of damage at a deep inner level.

It will become critical for you to break the chains of validation from unhealthy people. You need to put this pebble in your pocket and get to a place inside of you where you don't need unhealthy people to validate you on your path where you are, where you've been, or where you're going or who you're as a person.

It's a difficult pebble for me to keep picking up and I'm still constantly working on it because it's a necessary step for me to have peace and confidence.

Why is this important for you? It allows you to not be tossed about. It allows you to be grounded in truth: your truth. It gives you peace. It gives you freedom to not be tied down to other people's stuff and lack of ability. It won't affect you and thus it allows you to not be over reactive. Look to healthy people and your Higher Power to give you validation.

How do you break the chains of validation?

- **Find healthy people to seek validation from.** You'll not get validation from an addict that isn't in recovery. Like writing on a wall, you can read from their behavior whether they are in recovery or not. You'll feel it in your body.

- **How do you feel after you look for validation?** Do you feel shamed or blamed in your feelings? Do you feel like a big black coat is being taken off another and tossed on you? Or does it feel good inside you? Do you feel loved and accepted? Notice how you feel and that will give you good information to know whether it's a safe person to seek validation from.

- **Pinpoint the validation you're seeking. Is it something you can give yourself? If you can't give it to yourself, ask why?** Sometimes we're not able to give ourselves the validation that we desperately need. Why? Because we don't believe it and need others to help us see.

- **Is there anything in your core belief system that keeps you going to unhealthy sources for validation?** Are you in denial about the betrayal so you keep asking? Do you struggle to still look to the person who betrayed you out of habit?

- **Don't fight back when you don't feel validated.** When we don't feel safe, we go into fight, flight or freeze mode. Dr. Skinner has said that it's critical to not go into fight mode. If you can stay calm, then the focus can stay on their misbehavior. Although deflection may come, not reacting will help stay on the issue you're trying to discuss and help them see. If they can't see and you find yourself getting angry, stop the conversation and walk away.

"People whose integrity have not been damaged in childhood… they will use their power to defend themselves but not to attack others."[23]

- **Be assertive.** "Assertiveness makes clarity valuable. As a result, you'll be quite satisfied after an encounter with someone if you have honestly presented yourself and your position. Your satisfaction will no longer depend upon whether the other person acknowledged you or agreed with you. You'll no longer wish you said more. You'll have no need to correct people's impressions of you by going back to say more. 'I spoke in accord with the truth accessible to me at that moment and that is enough, even though I may have said it more effectively.'"

  "Assertiveness will feel fearsome and risky. Risk really means 'not in control of the outcome'. When you're assertive, you stop trying to control circumstances or other's behavior. When you're attached to staying in control, you're betraying the part of yourself that is fearless."[24]

In this chapter, we discussed how to break the need to seek validation from unhealthy people. In the next chapter, we'll discuss fighting back.

[23] Richo, David, and David Richo. *How to Be an Adult: a Handbook on Psychological and Spiritual Integration.* Mahwah, NJ: Paulist Press, 2018.
[24] Richo, David, and David Richo. *How to Be an Adult: a Handbook on Psychological and Spiritual Integration.* Mahwah, NJ: Paulist Press, 2018.

YOUR ACTION PLAN

Journal:

- What links are in your chain? What have been your patterns or beliefs in your marriage that make it difficult to not NEED your spouse's validation?
- Have you lost confidence in yourself?
- Have you lost confidence in your ability to make your own decisions?
- Are you afraid to make mistakes?
- Are you afraid to ask others outside of your spouse for advice?

Physical Action:

- Find a linked chain around your house or at the hardware store. Do the work to unlink the chain. What tools did you use to unlink that chain? How long did it take you? Did you get hurt trying to pull the metal apart?

Mental Action:

Repeat these affirmations morning and night:

I don't need my betraying partner to validate me.
I can validate myself.
I can find healthy people to validate me.

For the full list of affirmations, go to
https://beckyjonesbtcoach.com/freeactionguide

FIGHTING BACK

"**W**here was God in all of this? Didn't He care how His children were hurting each other?

It came to a head one day when I was looking out the window from a city bus. I saw a frustrated and tired mom yell fiercely at her son for doing something. When she turned her back to keep walking, the boy turned to his younger brother and hit him in the face. Such a small moment. Such an insignificant, mundane occurrence, but I sat there and cried. The smallest boy was so confused and hurt. I just wanted to jump off the bus and hug him.

The thing is, these were not bad people. They seemed representative to me of how we are all hurting, plagued by insecurities, failing energies, and unmet needs. But our response to these deficits can trickle down and have terrible consequences in the lives of others. How can we ever be truly free if all we do is react to the triggers of conflict, selfishness and competition all around us?" [25]

People do interesting things to take back power in their lives. Sometimes, to take back power, they hurt someone else. They're hurting, so they turn around and intentionally or unintentionally hurt someone else. Either way, it doesn't make it right.

---

[25] Robison, Becca. "Freedom: The Dignity of Our Own Choice." Small Seed. Small Seed, July 24, 2017. https://www.thesmallseed.com/blog/2017/07/freedom-the-dignity-of-our-own-choice.

A guiding principle that is important to recognize is that if I fight back with the intent to hurt someone, then I'm no different from the one who just hurt me because I would be reacting to my pain like they just did. Their initial pain/discomfort/frustration/addiction or poor coping habits and inability to sit in their pain caused them to hurt me. If I react and hurt someone else because of my pain, I'm no different. The cycle will just repeat itself. The problem with fighting back is that you just keep the cycle going.

I love the quote in the movie *Lincoln* where he says, "Shall we stop this bleeding?"[26]

I know you're hurting. I know it's the worst pain in the world. I know that anger is boiling up inside of you because of the inequities that happened to you but I want you to stop and think about what type of person you want to be.

Like the author said, other people's deficits trickled down into your life and had terrible consequences in your life. Don't repeat that cycle. Stop the bleeding. Don't be that kid who turns around and hurts someone else, no matter if it's the person who hurt you.

We all hurt others in our pain, even when we don't mean to in small ways and large ways. Sexual betrayal is a large way. But there are small ways we hurt others. For example, we may yell at someone when we're hurting. But practice makes perfect. If you're committed to learning to deal with your pain, how not to react and fight back, then you can become stronger in coping with the pain. You'll avoid being someone that you're not. And, using your relationship with your Higher Power, you can find that ability to not fight back.

We all hear the crazy stories about what people do for revenge. We laugh and think they're so crazy but if you've ever been in a situation where someone has hurt you so deeply, you may understand to a small degree why they do those crazy things.

For myself, I've experienced that pain makes you want to do things that you normally wouldn't do. It's a natural reaction to strike back and

---

[26] *Lincoln*, n.d.

"defend" yourself. I've experienced that it's hard to have self-control when I'm hurting.

I've made the mistake of fighting back at times. But it's a rock I've picked up on my road to healing. It's a principle that has meant so much to me because it's helped me step back and see it all, as if I'm watching a movie. Seeing it in a movie helps me feel empathy for all involved and gives me the strength to not make the same mistake. I won't fight back. I won't become someone that I'm not because of what someone did to me.

In this chapter, we talked about focusing on being our best self in painful situations and not fighting back. In the next chapter, we'll look at how to feel safe.

YOUR ACTION PLAN

Journal:

- What are ways you can take power back in your life?
- What is a reaction you've had in the past to someone who has hurt you?
- What reaction would you like to have when someone hurts you.

Physical Action:

- Remember a time when someone had hurt you. Go outside and go on a walk or do some exercise. Go punch a punching bag at a local gym. Get out all the anger you feel at their treatment of you. Now go back home and get out a blank piece of paper. Draw a mind map or a collage of all the choices you have right now in your situation.

Mental Action:

Repeat this affirmation morning and night:

I can acknowledge the pain but choose to act like my best self and who I want to be.

For the full list of affirmations, go to
https://beckyjonesbtcoach.com/freeactionguide

HOW TO FEEL SAFE

I'm from a small town: summer softball games, community Christmas tree lighting, main street trick or treating. I loved being in a small town until I found out about my husband's betrayal.

The cozy, friendly, safe environment I was used to turned into a war zone. Figuratively, I found myself on an open field with no cover, and the enemy was all around. I felt panicky. My heart raced. I felt extremely unsafe.

I would regularly face the reality of the sexual betrayal. The pain would plop itself down on my lap like a fluffy dog and just look up at me and laugh. I was puzzled at the clinical, sterile idea that the therapists would tell me that I needed a safe place to heal from betrayal trauma. There was no safe place in church, home, family, or community.

To make matters worse, everyone seemed to feel the need to take sides. Fingers were being pointed in every direction, including blame being assigned to me and the mistress's husband. Justifications that came from my husband's and mistress's mouth catapulted family and friends to follow their lead and betray me as well. Not only was it unsafe physically, it was unsafe emotionally as well. I was very unsafe at a core level. I had no one to protect me, no one to stand up for me. And other people's decisions thrust me into this place. The problem with betrayal is that it's hard to feel safe anywhere.

The only people I felt safe with were my children. They were the only ones who could see.

Though your situation may vary from mine, you're no doubt standing in a place of insecurity. You're surrounded by people you don't trust. You're surrounded by people who make decisions that hurt you. You're unsafe with the person who took a vow to protect you.

How do you feel safe?

- **Huge answers lie in the work of Sariah Bastian.**[27] She is amazing and recently wrote a book called "Beyond Breath." In her work she teaches you to find safety in your own breath, your own body and the ground beneath you, the earth that holds you up. She teaches you how to stay present, breathe, and ground yourself when you feel unsafe. Her book and Prana class[28] is a must for those seeking safety in an unsafe world.

- **What I do:** Finding safety for me looks like me closing my eyes, connecting to my breath, and breathing deeply. Breathing deeply slows my heart rate. Breathing deeply changes the fight-or-flight response in my brain. I feel the ground underneath my feet. When I'm in the middle of feeling panicked, feeling my rib cage expand helps my brain calm down and think clearer as I breathe in deeper.

At times, no matter what I do, I don't feel safe. All the tools and self-care I've tried don't work. My heart, body, and mind are screaming at me that I'm unsafe.

I listen to it

I validate it. I have a right to be in my own skin, meaning I have a right to feel the way I'm feeling and I validate myself.

I act. I do what I need to do to take care of myself and keep myself safe.

I have a right to feel safe.

Feeling safe regardless of my circumstances is a valuable rock I needed to pick up for myself. I can count on no one but myself to keep me safe.

---

[27] "Yoga Therapy; Betrayal Trauma and Addiction Recovery." Sariah Bastian. Accessed February 8, 2020. https://www.sariahbastian.com/.

[28] "Prana - Betrayal Trauma." Bloom For Women. Accessed February 8, 2020. https://bloomforwomen.com/prana-program/.

Sometimes, I'll need to make difficult decisions and have strong boundaries so I can feel safe. I have the right to feel safe and act in ways that will keep me safe.

In this chapter, we talked about feeling safe. In the next chapter, we'll be discussing blame.

YOUR ACTION PLAN

Journal:

- What circumstances make you feel unsafe?
- Whom do you feel unsafe with? Why?
- What actions can you take to help yourself feel safe?
- What can you change in your environment to help you feel safe?

Physical Action:

- Taking your list above of the circumstances that make you feel unsafe, make adjustments in your life that can help you feel safe. Do you need to block someone's phone number? Do you need to not go to a certain store? Do you need to redo your bedroom? Take physical action to do what you need to do to feel safe.
- Breath in and out. Feel the ground beneath your feet. Feel yourself in this moment. Feel safety in this moment.
- Order Sariah Bastian's book "Beyond Breathe" from Amazon.
- Sign up to take her Prana class from bloomforwomen.com

Mental Action:

Repeat these affirmations morning and night:

God hasn't abandoned me
I have a right to feel safe.
I breath in and feel the ground beneath my feet.
I am safe inside my own skin.

For the full list of affirmations, go to
https://beckyjonesbtcoach.com/freeactionguide

BLAME

Blame is a beautiful brown rock. It's smooth and glossy. When I step on this rock, it isn't hurtful at all. In fact, it's a bit soothing because it's so cold and smooth and feels gentle on my feet. This rock is scattered everywhere on my road to healing from betrayal trauma. I look down on that rocky road and there are so many glossy brown rocks. I turn in any direction and see that beautiful brown glossy rock.

Why is that rock everywhere? Because at every turn in my journey, I'll have the choice to blame others. It's the most common rock. It doesn't hurt me at all when I step on it. In fact, the glossy smooth rock feels good against my sore and bloodied feet. It's easy to hop down the road and land on these smooth brown rocks to avoid getting a cut on the other sharp rocks.

But this smooth glossy rock of blame is deceitful. It feels good but doesn't help me. I've learned that blame will keep me stuck. I won't heal with blame. Blame is like a beautiful brown coat that's full of holes. I can put on that brown coat, thinking that it keeps me warm, but it doesn't. I'm stuck in my own façade. I convince myself that this old, beautiful brown coat is keeping me warm. But it's not.

The problem with blame is that it's so easy to blame. It feels good to blame. It's true that we're here because of someone else's choices. But if we stay stuck in that whirlpool of thought, it's difficult to get out. Why? Blame keeps us stuck because our focus is on them and what they did and not on ourselves and getting ourselves out of where we are.

To forgive is to pardon an offense. It is to let go of blame for a past hurt. It is to release a great burden. It is to move ahead with life.

When we seek to place blame, however, we actually magnify our pain. This is because the act of blaming focuses our minds and hearts on the past, causing us to relive the hurt and harbor emotional and spiritual injuries that might otherwise heal. Resisting the urge to place blame is key to our ability to forgive.

In order to fully heal, we need to accept responsibility for our reaction to whatever happens. Taking responsibility for the condition of our hearts allow us to regain control of our lives. Although we cannot control what happens to us, we can always choose our response. Herein lies the power of our agency.[29]

I have so many betrayal trauma clients who are stuck. We can be stuck in a million different ways as we try to heal from sexual betrayal, but blame is a common place where clients are stuck. When we're stuck in blame, it indicates that we haven't grieved the loss and accepted it. I know you were betrayed. I know the landscape of your life changed because of someone else's choices, but it's important for *your* health that you accept it and then let it go.

Letting it go will bring you peace. It will give you freedom to not stay stuck in your story. Letting it go gives you power. You're not a victim but a victor.

---

[29] Counselor, James E. FaustSecond. "The Healing Power of Forgiveness." The Church of Jesus Christ of Latter-day Saints. Accessed February 8, 2020. https://www.churchofjesuschrist.org/study/general-conference/2007/04/the-healing-power-of-forgiveness?lang=eng.

What do you do when you're stuck in blame?

1. **Look at the grief cycle.** Is there anything that you haven't gone through in that cycle? "From the pit of deep admission that something is irrevocably over and gone, we finally stand clear of the insatiable need to find it again from our parents or partner. To have sought it was to have denied how utter was its absence! Grief work done with consciousness builds self-esteem since it shows us our courageous faithfulness to the reality of loss. It authenticates us as adults who can say YES to sadness, anger, and hurt. Such a heroic embrace of our own truth transforms emptiness into capacity. As Jung notes, 'your inner emptiness conceals just as great a fullness if you only allow it.'"[30]

2. **Do you think that blame will get you justice or recompense?** If we stop blaming, we feel that no one will see what a horrible person they are or what they did. It's a leap of faith to let blame go and see what doors will open in your life.

3. **When I want to blame others I either sing a song or repeat religious text in my head to help me.** Like water going down the same old ditch, blaming thoughts will creep in and run its course. If I'm aware and can see it happening, I can insert a song or religious text or think about something else to divert my thoughts. I love to repeat this poem when blaming thoughts come to my mind:

[30] Richo, David, and David Richo. *How to Be an Adult: a Handbook on Psychological and Spiritual Integration.* Mahwah, NJ: Paulist Press, 2018.

Invictus [31]

by William Ernest Henley

Out of the night that covers me,
Black as the pit from pole to pole,
I thank whatever gods may be
For my unconquerable soul.

In the fell clutch of circumstance
I have not winced nor cried aloud.
Under the bludgeoning of chance
My head is bloody, but unbowed.

Beyond this place of wrath and tears
Looms but the Horror of the shade,
And yet the menace of the years
Finds and shall find me unafraid.

It matters not how strait the gate,
How charged with punishments the scroll,
I'm the master of my fate,
I'm the captain of my soul.

4. **Focus on positives in your life.** I'll also try to combat blame by focusing on all the good things in my life. It's very easy to think about the bad things in your life; it takes discipline to think of the positives.

    The New Testament has the story of a blind man, about whom the question was asked, "Why is he blind?"

---

[31] Henley, William Ernest. "Invictus by William Ernest Henley." Poetry Foundation. Poetry Foundation. Accessed February 8, 2020. https://www.poetryfoundation.org/poems/51642/invictus.

"And as Jesus passed by, he saw a man which was blind from his birth.

And his disciples asked him, saying, Master, who did sin, this man, or his parents, that he was born blind?

Jesus answered, "Neither hath this man sinned, nor his parents: but that the works of God should be made manifest in him."[32]

I love this story. It reminds me of a different angle that I can see my bad life experiences from. I don't know why the man was born blind, but I do know that because of that, he was blessed with an amazing experience that few in this world have had: a personal healing from the Son of God himself.

I don't know why I was put in this position. I'll wear myself out if I focus on the why or blame others that this happened to me. However, if I can focus on all the wonderful "works of God" that are being manifest in myself, that helps me throw off the coat of blame and rejoice in the blessings that have come to me as I've worked on my recovery from betrayal trauma. I love my life now! If I'm hurting and want to blame others, I look at the specific hurt, why I'm feeling it, and take care of myself. When you blame, you relinquish your right to choose. Let go of blame.

In this chapter, we looked at blame and how blame can keep you stuck as you heal from betrayal trauma. Now, in the last chapter of the section of what pebbles you may need in your pocket at the beginning of your journey of betrayal trauma, we'll look at finding what you want.

---

[32] "Jesus Heals a Man Born Blind." Jesus Heals a Man Born Blind -. Accessed February 8, 2020. https://www.churchofjesuschrist.org/bible-videos/videos/jesus-heals-a-man-born-blind?lang=eng.

YOUR ACTION PLAN

Journal:

- Who is someone that you blame? Why do you blame them?
- How many times a day do you have blaming thoughts?
- In what ways does blame keep you stuck?

Physical Action:

- Put on an old pair of jeans that have holes in it. Are your legs kept from the weather? Why do you put on those holey jeans? Do they look cute? Are they cheaper to buy? Have you just had them so long that they wore out and got holes in them? If you compare the blame you have toward others to that pair of jeans, are there any new avenues of thought or insight that come up in your mind?

Mental Action:

Repeat these affirmations morning and night:

I can look for the good.
I will find joy around me.
I will let go of blame.

For the full list of affirmations, go to
https://beckyjonesbtcoach.com/freeactionguide

FINDING WHAT YOU WANT (IN THE BEGINNING)

Two chapters in this book are titled "Finding What You Want," one at the beginning and one at the end. Why? Finding what you want requires different information, depending on where you are in your journey.

When you first find out about the betrayal isn't a time to make any decisions. Why? See it for what it is: you're lying on a hospital bed, hooked up to monitors, and unconscious. The doctors and nurses are just trying to keep you alive.

From the ER bed, you move to the intensive care unit. There you're in and out of consciousness and managing your pain.

Honestly, it's difficult to find out what you want in the beginning because you're just trying to stay alive, manage the pain, and stay conscious.

There isn't a quick and easy solution after finding out about the sexual betrayal. There isn't a way to get the pain off quickly. If you can accept that fact, you might be more rash at figuring out what you want. Making a decision to go or stay doesn't take away from the work that you now need to do to heal. Sometimes, running doesn't make the pain go away. Sometimes, staying doesn't make the pain go away. The nature of your trial is just pain. Just accept that. Once you accept that, you can put it on the shelf and say to yourself, "Knowing that I'll have pain either way, what do I want." It's important to realize that your decisions may not affect your pain level. If you can accept that, what does that open up to you?

It will take time to figure out what you want. How to pick up the pieces of your life will come to you over time as you heal. Because it takes time, it's important to not look at your decisions as a way to control the pain.

Realistically, it doesn't make sense to make decisions at this point. Just focus on taking care of yourself, managing your pain, breathing, and staying safe. You don't have the strength yet to create a new landscape.

However, there's no road map for betrayal trauma. The greatest "roadmap" is the light that's inside you: your gut, your intuition. Listen to that above all else. Everyone's path is very different.

The main point is don't make decisions to just try to remove the pain. The pain is there and will have to be worked through, not walked around. Don't make the false assumption that if you stay or if you go the pain will subside. That's not true. Don't be hasty in your decisions to remove the blanket of pain.

Another point I want to make is to not be afraid to try on different "outfits." Imagine you were going to a clothing store and from the outside of your dressing room, people keep handing you different outfits. Some clothing you may think look good on the manikin, but don't look good on you. Some clothing pieces are, in your mind, not worthy to try on, but your store attendees urge you to try it and the outfit looks and feels great on you!

Life ebbs and flows as we try on different "outfits." However, we sometimes see it more permanent than that. If we see life as permanent, then we stop ourselves from trying on "outfits" or different ways of doing things. Don't be afraid to "try things on" in an effort to take care of yourself. Yes, there will be times you try it on and you don't like it, and that's okay. It doesn't mean it's wrong or you're a failure. It just means it wasn't the right fit.

In this chapter, we talked about finding what you want. We also finished discussing what may come to you at the beginning of your journey to healing from sexual betrayal. These lessons are difficult and hard, but as you scoop them up and put them in your pocket, you'll love what they will do for you, your life, and your ability to heal from betrayal trauma.

In the next chapter, we'll discuss what rocks will come up in the middle of your journey to healing from betrayal trauma.

YOUR ACTION PLAN

Journal:

- What do you want right now?
- What do you need to do to take care of yourself?

Physical Action:

- Book a hotel and just get away by yourself overnight. Just be with yourself. Go out to dinner with yourself, soak in the hot tub, watch a movie, read a book. What are some things that came up as you just took a break from dealing with the sexual betrayal? Did you notice anything you needed or wanted?

Mental Action:

Repeat these affirmations morning and night:

I can get the answers I need.
I can wait.
I can be patient in the pain.
I can be patient.

For the full list of affirmations, go to
https://beckyjonesbtcoach.com/freeactionguide

THE MIDDLE OF YOUR ROAD TO HEALING FROM BETRAYAL TRAUMA

I would define the middle of my betrayal trauma journey as I'm out of the Emergency room. I'm out of the intensive care unit. I'm out of the hospital.

This is the part of my journey where I'm walking on crutches. As far as the pain is concerned, I'm able to manage it with medication so that I can at least start to function again in real life. This is the part of the journey where I'm trying to get back to "normal life."

In the middle of my journey, I'm still navigating the unknown. I don't fully know what the extent of my injuries are and what they'll mean for my life. But I'm now facing the reality of what happened; I was hit by a truck and my life isn't what it was before.

I'll share these further lessons I picked up in this stage of my healing from sexual betrayal.

The first rock I picked up was about how to overcome shame.

OVERCOMING SHAME

Shame is a chunky and chipped brown rock. They blend in well with the brown dirt and there are so many of them. Their edges aren't sharp enough to draw blood, but I can uncomfortably feel four or five of these rocks under my feet every time I take a step. Those rocks are everywhere.

The problem with shame is that it shows up everywhere. Shame is a heavy dark feeling. It's deeper than a feeling like I've failed. It was that I was worthless. In betrayal trauma, it was hard for me to get away from that feeling. It. Was. Everywhere.

What is shame?

Shame is defined as "the painful feeling arising from the consciousness of something dishonorable, improper, ridiculous, etc., done by oneself or another. Shame is a painful emotion that responds to a sense of failure to attain some ideal state."[33]

Shame is the hardest thing to overcome because there are so many opportunities to feel it in sexual betrayal. It's still something I've yet to overcome but must watch for it lurking at the gates of my soul and squelch it before it comes in.

When did shame come?

---

[33] "Shame." Dictionary.com. Dictionary.com. Accessed February 8, 2020. https://www.dictionary.com/browse/shame.

Shame came:[34]

1. When someone said or did something: outside sources
2. Thoughts in my head because of the situation and how I felt about myself: inside sources.

I felt shame when people found out about the betrayal. I encountered many types of people. Some tried to comfort me and tell me it's not my fault. When those people wrapped their arms around me and told me it wasn't my fault, it felt really good. It was a gooey balm to my smarting and inflamed heart. It temporarily soothed the shame I felt. However, this balm is short-lived and can be potentially dangerous if I apply it too long. If I rely on others to soothe my aching heart over the betrayal, the more it stifles me to more forward into healing and shame-free living. I can't rely on others to stroke me and give me confidence. That confidence must come from within.

I felt shame when others would openly put the blame of what happened squarely on my shoulders so I swam in the shame of what other people put on me. "He wouldn't have done this if it weren't for you." At times, I could disconnect from the fact that they were talking about me and it got fun and interesting. As if I was watching a movie, people's deeply hid opinions now came spewing out of their mouths for my full enjoyment. Speaking in both anger and eerie calmness, they spoke as to how and why this happened to me. I wasn't a good wife. I was overreactive and emotional. I didn't give him enough space. The affair happened because we were having marital troubles. The blame that they put on me made it one of the most painful parts of the betrayal because I felt such shame. I didn't expect these ripple effects of other people's anger or opinions to hit me, as if I had the control over another human being's actions. They used carefully crafted words to

---

[34] "5 Factors That Make You Feel Shame." Psychology Today. Sussex Publishers. Accessed February 8, 2020. https://www.psychologytoday.com/us/blog/science-choice/201510/5-factors-make-you-feel-shame.

not own their own stuff but threw it on me. Shame was a great weapon for these types of people.

I felt shame when others would just turn and walk the other way and completely ignore me. This new development in my life made them feel uncomfortable. Whether they just didn't know what to do or say or whether they were wrestling with their own judgment, they found it easier to just turn their heel and ignore the fact that I even existed. It was hard to see people walk away from me. Their silence piled on shame exponentially because of the damaged lens that I viewed life from at that point. It was difficult to shake the idea that I really was a useless piece of crap.

I felt shame with thoughts in my own head. I had thoughts that I wasn't good enough, that I wasn't a good wife, that this was my fault. Shame came as thoughts went through my head as I searched for meaning as to what happened. The first thought that came was a tempting and logical thought, *This betrayal trauma happened to me because of my weaknesses and I wasn't good enough. If I was better or stronger, this wouldn't have happened.* This was a difficult thing for me because I felt like because I wasn't perfect, he left. I keep having to remind myself that no one is perfect but we can be perfectly committed to working through problems together. Finding solutions to marital problems outside of your marriage isn't really about me being perfect but the other person's coping ability. The truer, more accurate thought that barely passed through my brain long enough to remember it should be *This stuff happened not because of my weaknesses, but because of his weaknesses.*

I felt shame because of the situation I found myself in. I was left for another woman. He had a strong emotional connection with someone else that then turned into a physical relationship. They had a child together. Everyone in my small town knew about it. There pretty much was a sign on my forehead that said, "You're a loser wife." The situation brings so much heavy shame.

The problem with shame is that it can eat you alive and destroy you. For me, it eventually became like a hot potato in my hand; it hurt too much to hold it. It was too painful to regularly feel the sharpness against my feet as I stepped down on the chunky and ragged rocks of shame.

I turned and faced my shame. I was going to deal with it and face it head on.

I had to deal with two pieces of shame: other people's shame that they threw on me, and my own shame.

When other people have their own shame they haven't dealt with, it comes out on you. They turn to blame and anger when they don't deal with their shame. Anger is an easier emotion to deal with than shame. And blaming others is easier than looking at your own shame. This understanding helped when I felt shame from others. I could disconnect; it wasn't about me.

The main way I fortify against the shame that comes from others is to look at them clinically; they're just hurting over what happened, and their way of coping is to find someone to blame. If I can clinically look at them, I can give them the benefit of the doubt that it's their pain talking and they're taking their pain out on me. Again, when people can't deal with their own shame emotion, they turn to blame or anger. Those are easier emotions than shame.

Also, I try not to latch onto their story or assessment of me or what happened. It's very easy to spew out words without discipline. It's not a noble attribute to be able to do that. So, since it's so easy, I don't let it define me or latch onto what they're saying.

This is easier said than done. What they're saying hurts very deeply. It's difficult to not feel small and overcome by people who are opinionated and who judge. I've always struggled with people who speak well outwardly but use covert or direct comments laced with shame and blame to gain power over others. It may take me days, months, or even years to let go of the damage that someone's quick and undisciplined words can do. But I keep working at letting go of their story and their anger and blame. It's not mine! I'm tired of feeling shame!

Looking at my own shame involved me taking a hard look at myself. I started making mental notes of what brought the shame on. Just like pulling a loose string on a sweater, over time, I began to unravel where the shame kept coming from. Then I made a conscious decision to stay away from anyone, anything, or anyplace that brought on shame. Although I couldn't control everything and there would certainly always be unexpected encounters with shame, I did make an effort to guard myself against people, places, or things that I knew would bring it on.

The next thing I discovered was that my pride kept me stuck in shame. I cared too much about what people thought. I was stuck in a brutal washing machine cycle. I'll never heal in that place where I need someone on my hip all day telling me that I'm awesome and not at fault and a good person. It's not sustainable because when they didn't, I felt shame. What is sustainable is my own voice inside me taking responsibility for what's mine and letting go of what isn't mine.

Overcoming shame comes when my confidence starts coming back. My confidence starts coming back when I own and fix what I can fix. I can't fix someone else's porn problems or their desire to bat eyes with another person, but I can fix myself and take care of myself. Overcoming shame looks like me letting go of what isn't mine to own. Overcoming shame isn't being embarrassed by my trials but using them to serve others. That starts with me believing and knowing that I'm a good person, despite what happened to me.

Ultimately the shame I felt about myself healed when, through my religious practices of prayer, fasting, scripture reading, and temple attendance, I felt the undeniable witness from my God, my Heavenly Father of how beautiful, special, priceless and precious I am. I learned of my great value before my Heavenly Father and how much I'm loved. I received a witness that my Heavenly Father loves me so much and wants me to return to Him. He sent His Son to atone for my sins and through that atonement receive all that I need to be cleansed, healed, and enabled.

Overcoming my shame took baby steps. First, I had to pick up that rock, stare at it, and ask what purpose it served me. It wasn't serving me.

In this chapter, we just looked at how to overcome shame. In the next chapter, we'll look at following your truth and speaking your truth.

YOUR ACTION PLAN

Journal:

- What ways do you feel shame? Inside yourself and outside yourself?
- In what way does having shame hold you back from being the best you can be? How do you act when you have shame and when you don't?
- Why do others get angry with you or blame you? What could be their underlying shame that they haven't dealt with?

Physical Action:

- Go outside and sit in the sun. Feel the warmth of the sun on your skin and on your face. As you feel the sun on your face and skin, feel your Higher Power witnessing to you that you're His creation and that you're beautiful and loved. Sit there and just soak in that love. Whenever you need to get away from the feeling of shame, go back outside and sit in the sun.

Mental Action:

Repeat these affirmations morning and night:

I will let go of shame.
I will not let others throw shame on me.
I will work hard to guard against shame.

For the full list of affirmations, go to
https://beckyjonesbtcoach.com/freeactionguide

SPEAKING YOUR TRUTH.
FOLLOWING YOUR TRUTH.

True safety only comes by trusting yourself and honoring how you feel. One of the major causalities of betrayal is that you lose connection with yourself.

How do you lose connection with yourself? Because you're told constantly by your partner that your intuition is wrong. Your partner will do whatever it takes to keep their secrets safe. To keep their secrets safe, they need to attack the greatest beacon and homing device in the world: your intuition.

Over time, the bombs that your partner or spouse kept throwing at your beacon weakened it. How?

First, you start second guessing yourself. "Am I really feeling that?"

Secondly, you stuffed down your intuition like the candy wrapper evidence you stuffed down in the kitchen garbage can that no one would see. "Oh gosh, I really don't want to feel that right now."

Thirdly, you don't want to deal with the ramifications or consequences of your intuition. The conversation could go like the following.

"I'm feeling like something is wrong right now," you say.

"You're crazy and too sensitive. Why do you always have to be in my grill? You're like my parent," your partner says.

Feeling my truth and honoring that by speaking my truth became a very unsafe place for me. I was unsafe inside my own skin.

I had to relearn how to sit again in my intuition, feel comfortable with it, speak it, and be comfortable with the consequences.

It's a problem if you stop following your truth and speaking your truth.

It was an absolutely amazing experience for me have my royal robes back on my shoulder and my crown back on my head and to feel again how beautiful and important I was.

I could see in that moment the power and beauty of my confidence and certainty of what was inside me and how that scared others. I could see how others tried to talk me out of that and to protect their own truth by stifling me speaking mine.

Again, they would bomb the greatest beacon and homing device in the world which is your intuition.

My breath was given to me when I was born. I didn't put it in there on my own. It was given to me by my God, my Heavenly Father. It can be taken away at any time. Likewise, what was placed inside me was given to me: a light. It was placed there by God. That light would guide me. Thus, I had a divine right to be in my own skin and to be confident, to feel my truth and speak my truth.

A divine right to be in my own skin? I'm sure many of you are laughing at me. But it's true. We stifle our light, especially in betrayal, to make others feel comfortable. But in doing so, we keep ourselves stuck in the shame that they live in and the shame they want us to live in.

How do you get back to speaking your truth and following your truth?

1. **It will take time and a conscious effort.** You dug a rut over time with the water of your negative thoughts and energy, not knowing that you were hurting yourself. It will take time to recognize it and

dig a new and healthier channel for the water of healthy thoughts and energy to run into.

2. **Notice your habits. Change your habits.** You've slipped into habits that sabotage you speaking your truth and following your truth. What habits? You've learned to ignore it or stuff it down to protect yourself from the consequences that come with speaking your truth and following your truth. What consequences? Their anger, their shaming, their blaming, or any other hurtful action to keep you from talking about how you feel.

3. **Do imagery work to practice speaking your truth and following your truth**. It's important to mentally see yourself speaking your truth and following your truth. As you do this simple step, you'll see where you might slip and go into old habits because you're afraid or you want their love, validation, and acceptance. Then, in your mind, you can correct that sequence so you can then correct it in real life.

4. **Ask yourself what's holding you back from speaking your truth and following your truth**. You'll need to solidly and bravely face those reasons; otherwise, you'll keep spinning your wheels here. You may be afraid that they don't accept you or love you. You're right. They may not. But do they really love and accept you now or only when you make their life easier by ignoring their harmful behavior?

In this chapter, we looked at the importance of you speaking your truth and following your truth. It's an important step to look at *before* boundaries. Why? Because you need to heal and learn to trust your intuition because that will lay the groundwork for establishing boundaries. Now, in the next chapter, we'll discuss boundaries.

YOUR ACTION PLAN

Journal:

- What are you feeling?
- Why are you afraid to speak your truth?
- Why are you afraid to follow your truth?

Physical Action:

- Breathe in and out. God gave you your breath. It was given to you when you were born and it can be taken from you at any time. Breathe in and out very deeply. You have a right to be in your own skin. You have a right to feel what you feel. You have a right to speak how you feel and the truth inside of you.

Mental Action:

Repeat these affirmations morning and night:

I was given my breath by God.
I have a divine right to be in my own skin.
God will give me truth.
I can speak my truth.
I will not be afraid of how others receive my truth.

For the full list of affirmations, go to
https://beckyjonesbtcoach.com/freeactionguide

BOUNDARIES

n the "Finding What You Want" chapter, we talked about how we have to experience things or "try on outfits" to determine whether it's something we want to keep in our wardrobe.

Boundaries are the same way. We'll experience situations or feelings that feel good or bad. That sensory information is the blueprint to guide you where you should or shouldn't go.

Boundaries are defined as "guidelines, rules or limits that a person creates to identify reasonable, safe and permissible ways for other people to behave toward them and how they will respond when someone passes those limits."[35] They are built out of a mix of conclusions, beliefs, opinions, attitudes, past experiences, and social learning."

Boundaries are for us. We establish and maintain boundaries for ourselves. It's difficult to determine boundaries. It would be nice to hire a company that would print out a list of boundaries we should have, but sadly, it's only something we can do for ourselves. We have the responsibility to establish and maintain those boundaries for ourselves.

Boundaries aren't used to control other people. Rather, they make up a rule book for others to understand how they should interact with you and what you will and won't do.

---

[35] "Personal Boundaries." Wikipedia. Wikimedia Foundation, January 29, 2020. https://en.wikipedia.org/wiki/Personal_boundaries#cite_note-1.

Establishing boundaries was a hard pebble for me to put into my pocket. I avoided it. I was so used to letting others do whatever they wanted. I thought that was the nice thing to do and certainly a display of my religious beliefs of service. But that was a false framework that left me feeling like I had no choices or control and that I was powerless. When you're in that pot of powerlessness, anger becomes your fighting weapon because that's the only way you get people to back off and find any power.

Why are you scared to set boundaries with your spouse? In full transparency, I had a belief that marriage meant my spouse had all rights, privileges, and say over me, my actions, and my feelings. I mean we were supposed to be "one," right? It was a belief that was wrong and unhealthy and led me down a dark path.

When the betrayal happened, I knocked out the pillars of a false bridge of beliefs that I had built. The first pillar was that my husband absolutely had consecrated himself to me and had my back. With that pillar knocked over, I could clearly see he wasn't devoted to me or had my back, and it opened the way for the rest of my false supporting beliefs or pillars to also fall.

Those other pillars included that my husband had a right to judge me; I had no right to my own feelings, beliefs, and thoughts, even if they were different.

It was a beautiful time when those pillars of false belief crumbled and I became aware of my rights as a woman, wife, and human being.

I now felt completely free to set boundaries.

What do my boundaries look like? I froze when I was first asked that question by my therapist. I had no idea what I needed and I still was so unconfident inside of myself that I didn't believe I deserved any boundaries. That boundary question of what do my boundaries look like, sat on the shelf like a dusty book for a long time.

Then I started looking at boundaries from a different angle. What made me feel good? What made me feel bad?

Another way to ask myself was:

1. What emotion am I feeling?
2. Ask the emotion what it wants.
3. How can you get what the emotional wants through boundaries?

Also, did I need to protect myself from my own unhealthy behaviors I exhibited when I was treated a certain way by others? Did I need to protect myself from other's behaviors?

I'll give you an example of a boundary of mine. If I'm in a conversation with someone and I feel like they aren't listening but only shaming me and being passive aggressive, mocking, or criticizing, I'll end the conversation. Why? Because it protects me from getting angry and then getting desperate. In that place, I lose control because I don't do well when I'm being treated with these types of behaviors. Therefore, it's a boundary of mine that I won't play.

Another boundary of mine is that I'll protect at all costs the healing that I've received from the betrayal. If unhealthy relationships steer me back into shame, fear, or believing that I'm not worthy, I sever those relationships.

Boundaries are very individual. The best place to start is to follow that great light and homing beacon inside of you as to what feels good and bad. Start building your boundaries there. I promise you, like a road map, you'll be able to chart a course of great boundaries that will help you be your best person as well as keep you connected with healthy people.

In this chapter, we talked about boundaries. In the next chapter, we'll discuss how to work on your thoughts.

YOUR ACTION PLAN

Journal:

- Is there anything holding you back from setting boundaries?
- What emotion am I feeling? Ask the emotion what it wants. How can you get what the emotion wants through boundaries?
- What would you do if someone doesn't respect your boundary?

Physical Action:

- Put yourself in a safe place. Why do you feel safe there? What do you need to maintain that safe environment if the setting changes and the people moving in that setting change?

Mental Action:

Repeat these affirmations morning and night:

I can take care of myself.
I can learn what I need.
I can listen to myself.
I will know my boundaries.

For the full list of affirmations, go to
https://beckyjonesbtcoach.com/freeactionguide

HOW TO WORK ON
YOUR THOUGHTS

was caught in a loop. Like a bunch of open windows on a computer, my brain was constantly running in the background trying to figure out how and why this betrayal happened. My brain was constantly processing on who was right, who was wrong, who did what and why they did it. I was going over in my head my partner's story, their reasons and their why, and trying to make sense of it. Like a student surrounded by a bunch of open books and papers, I was searching everywhere, trying to find a story that my brain could put into a nice and tidy package to explain why this happened. I looped on this all day long, and it made me crazy.

When sexual betrayal happens, our minds need a story to latch onto. If our minds could have a story to latch onto, then we could start working the problem, right? If I had a story or the answer to "why this happened," then it could serve as a launching pad to propel me forward to heal, right?

But this isn't a true launching pad. In fact, this kind of processing makes you crazy.

Why?

First, other people's logical reasons for hurting you may not be full of truth. For example, what if your spouse said they betrayed you because you're emotional and angry a lot? Does that really provide a true launching pad for you to heal? Their logic was that "you were angry; therefore, I left you and formed an emotional attachment with another person and slept with them repeatedly." If you accept that as a true reason why they betrayed you, you could say, "Oh I'll work on my anger issues and then it'll all be better." But that's not a true launching pad because it really wasn't your anger that propelled them to form an emotional attachment to another person. You don't make someone do anything.

To accept that as the true story about why they did what they did will keep you stuck on owning stuff that isn't yours and you have no control over to fix.

Secondly, the most important reason why it's not a true launching pad is that it takes time and energy away from your main job at this point which is to focus on yourself and what you need to do to heal. Looping on who is right and wrong and why they did what they did exhausts your energy and keeps you in victim mode because your focus is on them and what they did to you and not on yourself. You need to focus on yourself to heal.

Like a truck stuck in mud, victim mode keeps us stuck. We're stuck when we focus more on the injustices handed to us and less on what we need to take care of ourselves and what we need to do to find peace. We push down on the gas pedal in our "truck" that's stuck, hoping that spinning the wheels will get us out. But instead, that digs us deeper and deeper into a rut. We need to stop and put pieces of wood under our tires so that we can pull ourselves out. We put pieces of wood under our tires by staying out of victim mode, working on ourselves, and focusing on ourselves. One of the pieces of wood I used to get my "truck" out was the book *Loving What Is* by Byron Katie. It was an empowering read because it allowed me to keep exploring deeper into myself and stay out of victim mode.

The work of Byron Katie is a simple process of questioning stressful thoughts. It's

> a way to identify and question the thoughts that cause all the suffering in the world. It's a way to find peace with yourself and with the world. Anyone with an open mind can do this Work."

I love what she said about this process: *"I understand the process of inquiry intellectually, but I don't really feel anything shifting when I do it. What am I missing?* If you answer the questions superficially with the thinking mind, the process will leave you feeling disconnected. Try asking the question and going deeper. You may have to ask the question a few times to stay focused, but as you practice this, an answer will slowly arise. When the answer comes from inside you, the realizations and shifts follow naturally.[36]

The first step is to identify specific thoughts that would come in my head. I would write them down. Then I would start picking it apart like I was doing a math problem.

The four questions are:

1. Is it true? *The answer to the first two questions is just one syllable: either yes or no. Be still and find your honest yes or no as it arises to meet the question. If your answer shows up as a yes, move to question 2. If it's no, then experience that no for a moment and then move to question 3.*
2. Can you absolutely know it's true? *If your answer to question 1 is yes, ask yourself: "Can I absolutely know that it's true?" Take this opportunity to look again. Shine the flashlight on that moment in time again, and see what reveals itself to you.*
3. How do you react, what happens when you believe that thought? *Close your eyes and witness the feelings, body sensations, and behaviors that arise when you believe that thought. Notice and report the answers to any of the following: What images do you see, past or future, and what emotions or physical sensations arise as you witness those images? How did you treat the other person? How did you treat yourself? Do any obsessions or addictions begin to appear when you believe that thought?*

---

[36] Katie, Byron, and Stephen Mitchell. *Loving What Is: Four Questions That Can Change Your Life*. New York: Harmony Books, 2002.

4. Who would you be without that thought? *Closing your eyes, return to the situation. Take a moment to reflect, observe, and experience the situation again, this time without the thought. Who or what you would be without the thought? How would you see or feel about the other person? Drop all your judgments. Notice what is revealed.*

5. Turn it around. Is the opposite as true as or truer than the original thought? *To do the turnarounds, find opposites of the original statement on your Worksheet. Often a statement can be turned around to the self, to the other, and to the opposite. Not every statement has as many as three turnarounds. Some may have just one or two, and others may have more than three. Some turnarounds may not make any sense to you. Don't force these.*

Finding the turnarounds were huge for me. They allowed me to dig deeper and really understand myself and my emotions. Working on my thoughts brought so much peace, clarity, and power.

In this chapter, I shared an idea from Byron Katie on how to work on your thoughts. In the next chapter, we'll discuss what the "end" of your road to healing from betrayal trauma looks like.

YOUR ACTION PLAN

Journal:

- Find the thought that keeps coming up that causes you pain.
- Answer the four questions on that thought and do the turn-around.

Physical Action:

- Go put on an outfit. How do you feel when you put on that outfit? Now, put on a different outfit. How do you feel in that outfit? Try again another outfit and see how that feels. Compare trying on outfits to trying on different thoughts. How do those thoughts feel? Is it easier to try on clothes rather than different thoughts? Why?

Mental Action:

Repeat these affirmations morning and night:

I can do the work on my thoughts.
I can do the work to stay out of victim mode.

For the full list of affirmations, go to
https://beckyjonesbtcoach.com/freeactionguide

THE "END" OF THE ROAD OF HEALING FROM BETRAYAL TRAUMA

There's no "end" to you working your recovery from betrayal trauma. I don't want to discourage or disappoint you by saying that. This isn't a hopeless statement. Why? Because part of the beauty of your journey is always working your recovery. You didn't come this far, having put beautiful pebbles in your pocket to just ignore them. Working recovery isn't like being on an endless treadmill that never stops. Working your recovery is like being in shape enough to walk into a gym and feel confident to use any machine and do any work out, feeling excited to get your heart rate up and better yourself. We've come so far at this point and learned so much that we don't want to stop.

This is the part of my journey where I'm looking for quality of life and peace. The pain, for the most part, is managed and I'm out and about in society and back to doing "normal" things. For the most part, I look normal. I don't use crutches to walk. No one would suspect that I had been hit by a truck.

True recovery means that I don't let this affect my life. I scoop up all the good and let the bad fall through my fingers. True recovery means I know how to take care of myself. True recovery means I have peace. Now we'll look at the ten pebbles I put in my pocket to help me sustain my healing and recovery from betrayal trauma.

You'll always have effects, but it doesn't mean it can or will take away your quality of life. You can have joy and so many good things. And who knows, maybe, in some ways, your life could be better now, if you're open to that possibility.

We just talked about what the "end" of your road to healing from betrayal trauma looks like. In the next chapter, and the first of the ten lessons we'll look at, we'll discuss why it's important to view betrayal trauma in the right framework.

FRAMEWORKS

As you're walking this road to healing from betrayal trauma, you'll come in contact with two models. I want you to be aware of those models: the codependency model and the trauma-based model.[37] These models are how others view and treat victims of sexual betrayal.

The codependent model is based on the idea that the partner of a sex addict is a person who has let another person's behavior affect them and they're obsessed with controlling them.

The trauma-based model is that you're a victim of abuse because of the lies, gas lighting, table turning, and blaming and that you're psychologically manipulated.

These are very different models, and you'll meet people and professionals who use one or the other. It's important to see it and call it what it is. These models lead to very different outcomes and feelings for someone trying to heal from betrayal trauma.

The codependency model is very harmful for those seeking to heal from betrayal trauma. It has been said by professionals that the codependency model is a form of victim blaming. It's also diagnostic mislabeling; they're taking someone who's been abused and has trauma from the abuse and mislabeling their symptoms and saying they have symptoms of a codependent and have a co-sex addition. In that way, they blame victims of abuse.

---

[37] "Why The Codependency Model Is Harmful To You | Betrayal Trauma Recovery." YouTube. Accessed February 8, 2020. https://youtu.be/epzxsrDp8kM.

Another harmful aspect to those who ascribe to this model is that they tell the partner who did the sexual betrayal to not tell their partner of the sexual betrayal, that it will harm them and cause them more pain. On a fundamental level, that's wrong. We have a right now know any information that affects our lives and our bodies. We have a right to any and all information about our health and our relationship. Transparency is right and important. And there can be no true connection without honesty and full transparency.

Another harmful aspect of the codependency model is that it draws a line between the addict's stuff and the partner of the addict. They advocate to the addict that it's their stuff; they don't need to tell their partner. Again, that isn't true. The partner of the sex addict has a right to know. It's not just their stuff at this point.

Another harmful idea of the codependency model is that the partner of the sex addict has a part to play in their addiction. That framework of a codependency model is incorrect. You're a victim and have no control over the choices of another.

We're uncomfortable still with emotional/psychological abuse. We're able to comfortably label physical abuse but we aren't as comfortable with emotional/psychological abuse. We struggle to say to those who are a victim of sexual betrayal they were abused. However, lying, gas lighting, table turning, blaming, and manipulation are all forms of abuse.

Because of the damage that the codependency model does to the partner who's been sexually betrayed, many professionals advocate for a trauma-based model both to treat the victim and to help the marriage. The research shows that a better outcome exists for victims of sexual betrayal using the trauma-based model instead of the codependency model both for the victim and for the victim's relationship, if it can be salvaged.

Because very different models are used to treat victims of sexual betrayal, it's important to know what framework they're operating in. This will have a great effect on your healing and the relationship's healing.

In this chapter, we discussed the framework that others view sexual betrayal in. In the next chapter, we'll discuss some long-term aspects to healing that will push and stretch you. You may hate me after this chapter.

YOUR ACTION PLAN

Journal:

- What model are you operating in?
- What model are the professionals who are helping you working in?
- What have you believed about yourself and your situation because of your partner's addiction?

Physical Action:

- Put a marble in a box and move the box around so that the marble slides around in the box. Now put the marble into a different box. Compare how different it is for the marble to be in both boxes. How is that similar to being in different thought frameworks? What does each box limit or open up to the marble? What does the framework that you're in limit or open up to you?

Mental Action:

Repeat this affirmation morning and night:

I am not a victim but a victor.

For the full list of affirmations, go to
https://beckyjonesbtcoach.com/freeactionguide

PUSHING AND STRETCHING

What I'll say in this chapter will stretch you. You may want to throw the book away after this.

Our goal is long-term recovery and healing from sexual betrayal. I'm sharing with you pebbles I put in my pocket that have helped me in long-term recovery that have brought me peace and quality of life. You may not feel that they are for you, and that's okay.

One day, I was sitting in the entryway of a lodge at a biking event I took my son too. I was hours away from home and we were camping in the mountains. Although I didn't have phone service, I used my phone to read and my battery was getting low. My search for an electrical outlet brought me to the entryway of the lodge. As I sat there charging my phone, doors would open and strangers would file through. My heart was so heavy and I'm sure my eyes were glistening from tears that were brimming. I felt in my gut the need for a good, hard cry. But the need to charge my phone kept me sitting in a place where I could be seen in my vulnerable state.

A lady, whom I had met once before but don't know her name, walked through the doors as I glanced up. Our eyes connected for just a second, long enough for her to know that I was hurting. She approached me with compassion and I felt at ease to open up. I told her what I was searching for. She then shared with me something so helpful that I'll never forget.

Our emotions often want to drive the car. Emotions are good and valid and have a place, but they shouldn't be driving the car. Our values and goals and beliefs should drive the car. Emotions need to be validated but seated in the shotgun seat of the car and not drive it. Our beliefs and values should drive the car.

What does this look like when people's choices hurt me? I may feel desperate, hopeless, angry, sad, wishing so much to be validated, alone, and in pain. However, those emotions don't need to drive my reactions. They are there and they are real but their proper place is next to the driver's seat and not IN the driver's seat. I need to put my values and my beliefs in the driver's seat. What do I value? What do I believe? Who do I want to be?

Who do I want to be? I want to be my best self regardless of what is happening around me. I want to stay grounded in who I am and not what others think I am.

What do I believe? I believe that other people's treatment of me doesn't define my worth. I believe that I'll be held accountable for my choices in how I react. I believe in treating others how I would want to be treated. I believe in loving my neighbor. I believe in being kind. I believe in having boundaries. I believe in taking care of myself, loving myself, and keeping myself safe. I believe in taking care of my anger in healthy ways but not stuffing it down nor lashing out uncontrollably.

What do I value? I value honesty and commitment. I want to be honest in how I feel and how someone else is making me feel. I want to be committed to myself.

These are the values and beliefs that need to drive my car. I may feel hurt by another but those feelings of pain and hurt can't drive the car. My values need to drive the car.

It was so important for me to let go of trying to control other people's choices that end up hurting me. In that place, I did desperate things I regretted. For me, regret looked like anger toward that person. Those reactions never helped. They hurt me and the people around me and took me farther from my goal of just wanting people to see me for who I was. That person also took my poor reaction to justify that I was deserving of their poor behavior toward me.

This is what I wish I would have known. I wish I could have seen those lines clearer. I lost myself. I lost control of myself. I lost focus on who I was. I lost focus on who I wanted to be. If I would have just let it go and focused on being the best me, I would have avoided pitfalls.

The truth is that people will only see you if they *want* to see you. You can't control that they see you. Besides, if they truly saw you, then they would have to change, and change is sometimes hard and uncomfortable; many would rather not do the work to change. It's easier to blame the other person.

So, as I let go of their choices and focused on my choices, values, and beliefs and who I wanted to be, I felt power and confidence filling back up inside me like a battery being recharged. I wasn't a victim. I was a victor. I had a choice in how I could react, respond, and be. The beautiful but hard pebble I put in my pocket was the power of choice and agency, the power of myself.

Now I'm going to throw another cog in the chain. If you haven't thrown the book out at this point, you may now.

At some point, you'll come across this pebble. I had to learn to stoop down and pick it up or I would fail. My journey would have gone a different way had I not learned to pick this up.

Sometimes a horse, even though you have a bit in their mouth and prompt them to turn, will just turn their head but their body is moving in the same direction.

So many times, I've wondered if I was like that horse, thinking that I had meekness and humility. Perceived humility is like that horse that turns their head but their body is moving in the same direction.

A good horse moves and bends according to their rider's command. A good horse gives to the bit and moves their body in the direction the rider wants it to go.

I found an amazing article that I read over and over again.[38] It was like a bit in my mouth, I found myself truly being measured to see if I really was bending. There were some powerful, strong points made where I could see if I was just bending my head or moving my whole body in the direction that my master rider, Christ, wanted me to go.

"The meek are urged to do good but avoid growing weary."

This is the last thing I want to hear.

I'm so tired.

I'm so tired of trying to be good when I don't feel like it's making a difference. They say that light dispels darkness, but I just feel like my little candle is about to be snuffed out in the vast darkness that surrounds me like a thick blanket. I believe that if you send out good, good will come back to you but sometimes it doesn't feel like that. You get tired because you don't see the fruit of your labors. You water the ground, thinking that flowers will spring up. But they don't and you sit there and stare at the ground and think that God lied to you. There's no fruit to your labors. Watering doesn't work. How do I not grow weary?

But maybe God's ways aren't our ways. What we think is going to happen isn't exactly what's going to happen. We think if we plant a seed and water it a flower will grow. We think if we're kind to someone, they will be kind back. That is the flower we seek and expect.

But God gave people their agency and choices. Doing something based on an outcome that someone else will change is a shaky foundation. Maybe God's intent is that we **become** regardless of what is happening around us. Maybe by sending out good, WE become the good. Maybe that's the intent of our God. By sending out good in the world, our lens is changed to see the good and we, therefore, see the good. If our focus is on our "flower" and that they will change, we might be disappointed and lose faith in the process. But if our focus is that flower that's growing and changing in ourselves, then we see and know that the formula works because we feel different, peaceful, and can act and not be acted upon.

---

[38] Maxwell, Neal A. "'Meek and Lowly' - Neal A. Maxwell." BYU Speeches. Accessed February 8, 2020. https://speeches.byu.edu/talks/neal-a-maxwell/meek-lowly/.

Like water off a ducks back, you have to have the ability to not harbor resentment when good from others doesn't come back to you. It's hard not to grow weary of doing good unless you take your mental state to the next level. You need to know and believe that your God, not others, will give you the capacity to love and serve. Think about it; if our capacity comes from other people recognizing us, that really does limit us. But if you lean on God to give you that capacity to love and serve, your inner well will never run dry. And that God will feed you in the wilderness and in your famine. That's the food that lasts anyway, not the praise of recognition from others. Love and gratitude from God will last. That's how you not become weary from doing good. He also says, "You're not just worshiping your God but trying to be like him." Bending your whole body to the bit and turning and not just turning your head. Seeking recognition from others is "strength sapping." It's not sustainable to seek recognition from others.

"Meekness speaks the truth but speaks it in love."

I cannot claim to have this virtue all the time. When I'm at my end or the other person, I'm speaking to isn't listening, my voice is raising and I find myself yelling instead of speaking my truth. But that's what meekness looks like.

I get so disappointed in myself when it accelerates to that point. Why can't I stay calm? I think it's because my defenses are up and I see them as the enemy, not as a child of God. I think it's also because what they're saying pokes at things inside myself that hurt. To validate myself, I need to stand up for myself and speak my truth. But, instead of it coming out as "I feel," it comes out as "you did this," "you are."

How difficult this is when you want to tell someone your truth, that what they're doing is hurting you and they need to stop. It's hard to even feel love in your heart for the other person when you're trying to get them to lay down their weapon. My natural reaction is to speak forcefully like a cop to a criminal, "Put your weapon down!"

I don't even know what to tell you here except when you speak your truth, speak it with the image in your mind that you love yourself. Don't have the image in your mind that you're speaking to the enemy and demanding they put down their weapon down, but focus on the image that you love yourself. You can speak the truth in love about yourself and how you feel. You can't speak the truth in love about someone else and why they're doing what they're doing. You're on shaky ground because then your words can bleed into shame and blame toward them. And they definitely won't lay down their weapons then.

"Be devoted to God's cause but be prepared to sacrifice all things, giving if necessary the last full measure of devotion."

Have you heard this story from C. S. Lewis? "Imagine yourself as a living house. God comes in to rebuild that house. At first, perhaps, you can understand what He's doing. He's getting the drains right and stopping the leaks in the roof and so on; you knew that those jobs needed doing, so you're not surprised. But presently He starts knocking the house about in a way that hurts abominably and doesn't seem to make any sense. What on earth is He up to? The explanation is that He's building quite a different house from the one you thought of, throwing out a new wing here, putting on an extra floor there, running up towers, making courtyards. You thought you were being made into a decent little cottage, but He's building a palace. He intends to come and live in it Himself."

I feel like I'm devoted to God but when walls start getting torn down inside my house and I'm in pain, the pride kicks in to stop and I throw my fist up to Heaven and say this has gone too far.

I'm devoted to a cause until a certain point, but when huge abnormal amounts of pain are required, I want to throw up my hands and say, "No way, I'm out."

This is where our faith in God is tested. It's also easy at this point to look around and say, "You don't require this of others, why me?" or to say, "I don't really need to make the sacrifice, I've done enough." It takes meekness to say that I'll bend and bow to whatever you see fit and whatever cost.

It takes meekness to sacrifice those things within ourselves that we need to. Pride pushes back the pain of remodeling and justifies that the wall really doesn't need to come down. "It has served me well," I tell God. Yet the wall must painfully come down. God tells me, "I promise it will bring you peace and happiness." But it's hard to trust that it really will, especially when you're dealing with the pain of betrayal trauma. It's hard not to seek justification over sanctification.

"We are not only to forgive but we are to forgive 70x7." I must say that this element of meekness is so exhausting, especially when hurtful stuff happens over and over again.

I can confidently say in the arena of betrayal trauma, I've learned to not be surprised by what people say or do. People act and don't think things through. Others will cause you pain. The hardest thing is to forgive them once, let alone 70x7.

I was told in a blessing that other people's choices would cause me much harm and damage. That statement has been so true. People's choices will hurt you. They'll cause you damage. They'll cause you harm. But you have to keep forgiving and letting it go. There's no other way. Let it go and say to yourself, "let God judge between me and thee."

"Do what is right and do it for the right reasons." This statement cuts me to the core. I look at myself and say I'm doing the right things in my life. But, then to ask myself the deeper question of what my motive is for doing those things. Do I want to look good? Cleaning out the closet of all the real reasons why you do what you do is healthy.

You may find that your reasons in doing the right thing comes from a faulty, unsustainable place. If your reason is to look good and to save face, it won't be sustainable because that's a moving target in itself. Trying to please other people or look good is a moving target.

"We cannot make a new heart while nursing old grievances."

"Meekness also protects us from the fatigue of being easily offended. Meekness also contains a readiness that helps us to surmount the accumulated stumbling blocks and rocks of offense; we can make stepping stones of them and achieve a deeper and broader view of life."

If you're feeling like you can't breathe right now and you're so angry with me, that's okay. Others felt the same way.

"From that *time* many of his disciples went back and walked no more with him. Then said Jesus unto the twelve, Will ye also go away?" (John 6:66-67)

In this chapter, we talked about principles that require you to really stretch yourself but will lead you to greater freedom and peace in your life. In the next chapter, we'll talk about what it looks like to show up.

YOUR ACTION PLAN

Journal:

- What thoughts came to you as you read this chapter?

Physical Action:

- Go on the Internet and study the feathers on a duck. How do those feathers keep the duck warm and dry despite it living in the water? How are they easily able to dry off after being in the water? How does the water "roll off a duck's back"?

Mental Action:

Repeat this affirmation morning and night:

I can let my values and who I want to be drive my "car"

For the full list of affirmations, go to
https://beckyjonesbtcoach.com/freeactionguide

IT'S WHAT IT LOOKS LIKE TO SHOW UP

Basketball season was starting for my son's basketball team. Normally, it was an exciting time for me. I loved going to his games and watching him play. However, this year was different. People who were unsafe and triggering would also be at the games. It was another place I was no longer safe. It was another battle zone.

I went into my therapist and asked him to help me brainstorm how to walk through this triggering situation. He said something that was a powerful, reframing for me.

"Becky, this is what it looks like to show up."

Brené Brown has some amazing thoughts on vulnerability and "showing up."[39]

Most of us, when facing betrayal trauma, or any type of trauma, would like to curl up in a ball and never leave that fetal position. It's easier to just keep everyone out and not deal with it. Unfortunately, I can't do that. I have kids. I have a life. I can't just hide out forever, even if I think it would be safer for me.

---

[39] Brown, Brené. "The Power of Vulnerability." TED. Accessed February 8, 2020. https://www.ted.com/talks/brene_brown_the_power_of_vulnerability?language=en.

I needed to figure out how to not go into that survival part of my brain that panics when certain situations come up. How do I *override* my natural responses so I can show up?

"Becky, this is what it looks like to show up. It's going to be difficult but that's what it looks like to move through this. This is what it looks like to show up rather than stay home and hide."

Unsatisfied, I furrowed my eyebrows and glared at my therapist. "That's easier said than done," I quipped back at the therapist.

"The devil is in the details so keep just noticing how you feel and don't try to solve it. Anytime you slip into trying to solve it, you slip into panic and survival mode." What the therapist said hit me like a smack in the face. Resolution and acceptance filled my soul like water seeping into my boots when stepping into a river.

I didn't need to solve anything. I just needed to move through it and notice what it looked like to show up there in an unsafe place.

What does that look like? That looks like me walking into the gym and recognizing that my heart was racing. I could see I was having a physical reaction. As I walk past the unsafe person to get to my seat in the gym, I just tell myself it's normal to feel this way and this is what it looks like to be here and not stay home. Also, in that moment, I don't need to fix how I feel. There's nothing to solve because that's how it looks like to walk past that person. Trying to solve or fix that moment makes it worse. When thoughts came in to hijack my brain, I don't try and fix it. However, I may need to remove myself from the situation to "fix" it for me.

Here is where I noticed something cool about myself. My confidence started growing as I realized that these emotions were natural because I was showing up and I didn't need to fix anything.

It was going to be hard. It was going to be uncomfortable. My heart was going to beat out of my chest in those situations. But that's exactly what it looked like to show up.

I wasn't at home.

I wasn't in bed.

I was here. At my son's basketball game, watching him play.

At this point, I could see that my uncomfortableness didn't mean I needed to stop. It meant I was moving through hard stuff and not letting other people's harmful choices define my life.

I was showing up.

In this chapter, we talked about what it looks like to show up in betrayal trauma. In the next chapter, we'll talk about vulnerability.

YOUR ACTION PLAN

Journal:

- What are you doing in your life to show up, even though it's very uncomfortable?

Physical Action:

- Go in a safe place, like your room and see yourself showing up in an uncomfortable space in your life. How does your body feel? What are your emotions? Don't try to fix it but just notice yourself and what happens when you go in those uncomfortable spaces.

Mental Action:

Repeat this affirmation morning and night:

I can show up in hard places and do hard things as I live my life.

For the full list of affirmations, go to
https://beckyjonesbtcoach.com/freeactionguide

VULNERABILITY

While walking along my path, I stepped on a teeny sharp rock. It was glossy, gleaming, and beautiful. However, acute and cuspidate corners pricked my feet and they started to bleed. The puncture from the rock hurt deeply. I started to cry and lunged down to throw the rock. But the rock quietly spoke to me, "Don't throw me away. You need me to feel better."

I looked at it and laughed. "How could I need you? You're just another rock that causes me pain. In fact, you cause deeper pain than most of the other rocks. You're pointy and sharp. I don't need you.

But again, as my elbow was cocked and ready to throw it, the rock said to me, "You need me to heal. I'm the birthplace of change."

Vulnerability is the birthplace of change. With vulnerability, I can create something that wasn't there before.

Most people view vulnerability as a weakness. But, according to Brené Brown, "Vulnerability isn't a weakness."[40] but is allowing yourself to be exposed to the possibility of being attacked or harmed, either physically or emotionally. "Vulnerability is the willingness to say I love you first. To try when there are no guarantees. To invest in something that may or may not work out."

---

[40] Brown, Brené. "The Power of Vulnerability." TED. Accessed February 8, 2020. https://www.ted.com/talks/brene_brown_the_power_of_vulnerability?language=en.

This statement reminds me what Christ taught when He told us to turn the other cheek when someone hits you, to go the extra mile, to give someone your cloak when they just sued you for your coat. You're exposed when you act first and don't know how it will turn out. It's very vulnerable to stick your neck out for someone not knowing if they'll do the same for you or if it will come back to you. Vulnerability is being your best, regardless of how another receives it.

Brené Brown clearly spells out that to have vulnerability, you must have courage. I would add that I think to have vulnerability, you need to have a strong sense of who you are. Both of those: courage and knowing your individual worth aren't easy abilities. Vulnerable people aren't weak. Vulnerable people see clearly the choices before them, but with courage and faith, they choose to go through the hard to get to the best.

Vulnerability is also the capacity to expose myself. That's scary, but until I let down those heavy iron gates that have protected me, nothing can go in or out of my soul. For healing to take place, things must go in and out of those rusty iron gates.

Being vulnerable looks like me exposing myself to pain but it also exposes me to the possibility of joy. Being vulnerable in a relationship looks like me allowing a chance for repair and healing. Being vulnerable looks like me stepping away from other people's stuff that keeps me down, opening up new ideas, creating something new as I leave behind what I thought was safe, not fighting back in anger, and changing the ways I've protected myself.

I have had to be vulnerable to heal. It was the scariest thing in the world to do after I had been betrayed. In my situation, I had built walls and defense mechanisms to keep me safe from the betrayal that happened and the behavior that led to the betrayal. The vulnerability rock told me I had to tear down the walls and defense mechanisms if I wanted to heal. That rock told me that the walls and tools I had used before weren't useful now. I needed to change the ways I protected myself.

I was angry at first to the idea that I was the one who needed to change. I had built walls because I had an enemy. I had built those walls because

I wasn't safe. This rock quietly and painfully reminding me it was time to take down the walls was cruel and difficult. My foot bled, and I couldn't believe that there could be so much asked of me from a tiny, beautiful rock.

I had built walls of fear, reactiveness, disrespect, anger. Why did I build those walls? I built them because I didn't feel safe, understood, listened to, empathized with. I lacked a connection with someone who I thought cared about me. I felt scared. I felt like my life was out of control. I also felt alone because no one would help me. I felt gas lighted. I felt cast aside. I sensed things were wrong, but I was labeled as "crazy."

Until D-Day came, I didn't realize how much of a war zone I was in.

So here I was walled up in my castle. There was an enemy at my gates but I kept the enemy out by hunkering down in fear and pretending nothing was wrong. I kept the enemy back with reactiveness and throwing back the same hand grenades the enemy was throwing at me.

And that's when this little vulnerability rock says, "Open the gates. In fact, take down your walls. And while you're at it, disarm all your weapons."

Brené Brown says that we numb vulnerability. That is so true. I thought that there was no way that I was going to open the gates, take down my walls, or disarm my weapons with the trauma and betrayal that I had happen to me. I had a right to stay walled up behind all this stuff I built because someone hurt me. But she said in doing so you also numb joy and love with it.

This scripture came to me at the beginning and gave me a new battle plan. I didn't need to add any more fear or expectation on me. I could simply be the me I was made to be. This scripture told me to put down the walls and open up and don't be afraid.

"Fear not to do good, for whatsoever you sow, that shall ye reap."[41]

What did I want to reap? I want to reap goodness. I wanted to heal. I didn't want to feel afraid. I wanted be me. I wanted to be the person I was meant to be: unaffected by others' opinions or treatment of me and go for-

---

[41] "Doctrine and Covenants 6:33." The Church of Jesus Christ of Latter-day Saints. Accessed February 8, 2020. https://www.churchofjesuschrist.org/study/scriptures/dc-testament/dc/6?lang=eng.

ward and fulfill the mission I was sent here to do. I've got to open the gates. I've got to open up to the beauty that's out there beyond my iron walls.

Being vulnerable doesn't mean that I leave myself open to attack. I think that's the first response from most people. They want to slap a bad label on this principle. People rise up in anger because they think vulnerability is me laying down and being slaughtered. It doesn't mean that at all. I still protect myself, but I change it into ways that really do keep me safe and not just give me the illusion of being safe.

I can have peace in times of war. I can also have the absence of peace even when there's no war. I'll go into that in the next chapter, but I can be properly protected so that I can have peace even when war is raging around me. I can still have walls to protect me, but they must be the right kind of walls that won't barricade me in while I starve to death, that still allow safety and flow but are solid enough to add protection.

When I want things to change, it involves a change of course, which involves a new way. Changing the ways I protected myself into healthier ways keeps me feeling in control. Healthy ways help me detach from someone else's craziness. Just because they threw a bomb at me, doesn't mean I need to react and throw one back. I don't need to become crazy too.

It was healthy for me to own that my old ways of coping and defending myself were built because I was misinformed and uneducated about who the enemy was. Being honest about the circumstances in which I formed those unhealthy ways of coping and the lack of knowledge I had when I formed those old walls and weapons is important. I needed to forgive myself for turning into someone who I really wasn't and let go of the past.

Why would I want to look at myself so vulnerably? Because I'm tired of spinning in the same pile of crap and reacting to others' crap. I want to be free to be the divine self I was made to be. I'm tired of being afraid of what they'll do next. I want a better life than what I was pulled into because of someone else's choices. I'm tired of being walled up in my castle and being too afraid to come out.

Of course, bringing down my walls still does make me vulnerable. The other party often sees that I'm not in a defense stance, and they move in with sarcastic and demeaning comments. Or they might just openly ridicule me. They usually strike when my defenses are down because they see it as a time I'll think about what I'm doing wrong and change. Some people like to see me crying because they see it as humility.

But I have to resist the urge to go back to what it was before. I have to believe that my path is the right path and what it was before wasn't safe or healthy. I'm doing this for myself and not for them. They had power over me before. Now they won't.

How do I know that my walls aren't healthy? The goal is to be my best self. Anything that takes away from me being my best self needs to be looked at.

How do I know what those walls need to be changed to? I know through trial and error, asking questions from others on how they handle situations, reading books, and looking for new ideas on how to handle situations. Most importantly I look inward and to ask myself the hard questions as to why I do what I do. That deep and inward soul searching yields the greatest insights if we can be honest with ourselves.

A lot of insights came to me that I couldn't do for a while after I received them. I had a thought come to me several times of something I should let go of. God dangled it before me like a toy before a cat, trying to nudge me in that direction. I tried and failed and would try and fail again. I couldn't do it! But I stored it in my heart until I knew I was strong enough to be able to attempt to try it again.

If I couldn't do what God showed me I needed to do, I did ask myself why I couldn't do it. As I faced the reasons why I couldn't, I found myself staring at the vulnerability rock again.

I'll be vulnerable and share an example with you. I felt God asking me to let go of my need for understanding. I craved to be understood by others. I craved to be understood by my spouse. I craved to be understood by people in the community.

In that place, because it was so important to me, I began to try and force others to understand me. My plea would come out desperate, demeaning, and full of blame. Instead of getting the understanding and compassion I craved, my desperate attempt to get them to understand only justified their response. They either left me alone or were angry.

To heal, I had to be vulnerable and let go of the need to be understood. This left me unprotected in my greatest fear, that I wasn't WORTH being understood, that I wasn't worth the time or investment or energy from them to understand me. I was too much for them. I was "high maintenance." I now stood naked in front of my greatest fear.

But as I faced that fear, I saw that their view of me or investment in me had no reflection of my own value. It just was a reflection of their own inadequacies and abilities. Some people have the gift to see others as they truly are. That gift is called charity. It only comes to those who do the hard work to be able to have charity. Few people seem to have the desire to work that hard. That doesn't mean that I'm not worth it. It just means they can't.

I also realized that my need to be understood had its core roots in pride. Caring more about what other people think than we care about what God thinks is pride. I had pride. I knew God knew the circumstances, but I wanted everyone else to know. That was pride. I had to repent of the pride I had of looking good and caring about what other people thought because that took me away from being my best self.

Being vulnerable and facing my walls allowed me to understand my walls and take them down. Those walls weren't really safe. They were keeping me stuck in my fears and pain and not allowing me to be protected in the right and safe way. The right way to be protected is to know that I have so much worth and not confuse my value with others inabilities.

This little rock is both beautiful and painful. You'll come upon it at some point as did I.

Being able to be vulnerable takes time. Be patient with yourself. You'll know, as did I, when it's time to pick this rock up.

In this chapter, we talked about vulnerability and how it can help us in betrayal trauma. In the next chapter, we'll look at having peace despite what's around you.

YOUR ACTION PLAN

Journal:

- What are ways you've protected yourself in betrayal trauma? Have these coping mechanisms been healthy?
- Is there something you need to be vulnerable with that's holding you back from healing?
- Do you feel awkward being vulnerable?

Physical Action:

- The intent of this short, exercise is to physically demonstrate in a simple way, how hard it is to change our habits and how it feels when we're vulnerable and try something new or different. Hold your hands out in front of you and clasp them together with your fingers interlocking. Look at your hands and notice where your thumb and pinkie are. Now unclasp your hands and switch where you originally put your thumb and pinkie. Does that feel weird? Why did you clasp it the original way? Was it wrong or right to clasp it either way? Without even knowing our patterns, we do things a certain way. Sometimes we have reasons why, and sometimes we don't. When we decide to change those ways, how does it feel?

Mental Action:

Repeat this affirmation morning and night:

I can take down the walls that are keeping me stuck in my fears.

For the full list of affirmations, go to
https://beckyjonesbtcoach.com/freeactionguide

PEACE DESPITE WHAT'S AROUND YOU

n betrayal trauma, peace seems like it will never come. You're navigating a world where other people's pain and choices plop themselves on your doorstep and don't go away.

However, we can have peace even when there's a war around us. Sometimes, we don't have peace even if peace is around us.[42] It's a promise from God that we can have peace if we seek it. Peace comes from God.

"Peace is the gift of God. Do you want peace? Go to God. Do you want peace in your families? Go to God. Do you want peace to brood over your families? If you do, live your religion, and the very peace of God will dwell and abide with you, for that is where peace comes from, and it doesn't dwell anywhere else."[43]

Peace cannot be made up. We can talk ourselves out of anxiousness or worry or try to tell ourselves to feel better, but true peace comes from God. Sometimes, it's so subtle. We kneel down in pain and anxiousness then stand up feeling calm and relieved. We almost have to stop our-

---

[42] "Peace." The Church of Jesus Christ of Latter-day Saints. Accessed February 8, 2020. https://www.churchofjesuschrist.org/study/manual/true-to-the-faith/peace.html?lang=eng#title1.

[43] Eyring, Henry B. "Creating Peace: Blessed Are the Peacemakers." BYU Speeches. Accessed February 8, 2020. https://speeches.byu.edu/talks/henry-b-eyring/blessed-peacemakers/.

selves and recognize that God gave us peace. God gave us what we needed and asked for.

Many times, pure, unmanufactured peace came to me. At times, I knelt in prayer, desperately bowed in grief and pain, and a warm feeling of peace came in my heart. It wasn't something I could manufacture on my own. It was real, and it confirmed to me that God was in Heaven and heard my prayer.

I was touched when I heard from a friend who talked to God all the time that He was her best friend. I wanted to have Him as my best friend, too. Whether I prayed in my mind or knelt down, I wanted to develop that habit of turning to Him and talking to Him so often and making Him my best friend.

Peace comes as we travel away from sin. "No road leads to peace, for a person or for the world, unless it leads away from the effects of sin and Satan."[44]

Peace comes as you do the work you need to do to become a better person, to repent of your sins, to become like Christ and God. That work will bring you peace. Regardless if someone else chooses to do the work, you can still have peace in the work that you're doing.

"And it came to pass that the Lord said unto me: If they have not charity it mattereth not unto thee, thou hast been faithful; wherefore, thy garments shall be made clean. And because thou hast seen thy weakness thou shalt be made strong, even unto the sitting down in the place which I have prepared in the mansions of my Father."[45]

It's easy in betrayal trauma to get sucked into their world. It's also easy to not focus on the work that you need to do. Doing YOUR work will bring you peace. It will help you feel empowerment. I truly believe that as

[44] Eyring, Henry B. "Creating Peace: Blessed Are the Peacemakers." BYU Speeches. Accessed February 8, 2020. https://speeches.byu.edu/talks/henry-b-eyring/blessed-peacemakers/.

[45] "Ether 12:37." The Church of Jesus Christ of Latter-day Saints. Accessed February 8, 2020. https://www.churchofjesuschrist.org/study/scriptures/bofm/ether/12?lang=eng.

we become like Christ and draw closer to Him, we can have peace regardless of our circumstance and we can stay safe underneath His wing.

In this chapter, we talked about the need to seek peace from God for yourself. In the next chapter, we'll discuss the double-sided coin.

YOUR ACTION PLAN

Journal:

- What are ways you need peace in your life?
- Have you felt peace after you found out about the sexual betrayal?
- What are your roadblocks to peace?
- How do you find peace when other people's behavior affects your peace?

Physical Action:

- If you have a Higher Power, go and connect with Him right now. In whatever form or manner that you pray to Him, do so. If you don't have a Higher Power, find a quiet place to connect to your breath.

Mental Action:

Repeat this affirmation morning and night:

I can seek for peace for myself from the source of peace.

For the full list of affirmations, go to
https://beckyjonesbtcoach.com/freeactionguide

THE DOUBLE-SIDED COIN

My mind had been spinning the same story in my head. It was a horrid loop that I couldn't get myself out of. I was ready to heal. I was tired of hurting. But, like a computer that's running so many programs and has so much background noise, my brain was still trying to figure out why this betrayal happened. I couldn't make sense of it. I was exhausted. These thoughts were constantly running in the background of my mind and were with me in everything that I was doing.

Our brains need a story, something to latch onto. I could find no resolution. It not only drained me but was causing me to drift away from the peace and strength I needed. Like a battery that has a loose connection somewhere, I had to work harder to just keep functioning mentally. Something needed to change. I couldn't keep going on like this. I needed help but didn't know what I needed. I was hurting so bad inside that I told God I'm done, I can't do this anymore; take all this turmoil out of me, even if you need to cut it out.

One night, I was driving back home with my daughter from her soccer game. It was a 2-hour drive home, and we were driving in an area where there was no cell service. Suddenly, I felt a snap, and the car started losing battery power. Somehow my battery was draining fast. My daughter and I were on a windy mountain road that hosts a lot of trucks and there isn't a wide area to move off to the side. I panicked and started praying out loud to my Heavenly Father. "Father, what do I do?" I kept driving as the lights on my car got dimmer and dimmer. I just prayed and hoped I could get to a place that I could get off the road before I fully lost my lights.

I didn't realize until later that my car and I were on a parallel journey. My car needed lights and was failing because of a short circuit on the inside of the car. It was draining fast and rapidly losing power. Soon the darkness would overtake my little car. I was on the same journey. Although I tried to power my batteries each day through prayer and scripture study, I was losing power fast because of some short circuits in my head. I was lost and knew I was lost but didn't know how to help myself keep going on my journey in the darkness. But as always, a merciful Father in Heaven knows when you're lost and will always find you.

A merciful Father in Heaven guided me perfectly to a restaurant in the middle of that mountain highway. Amazingly, my lights went out completely just as we pulled up to this restaurant. The restaurant was closed but there were lights on inside. I pulled over as far as I could off the road and by a big light. My daughter and I knocked on the old wooden door. A round man with a thick white beard and a woman came to the door. I explained my plight to what looked like Santa Claus and Mrs. Claus and they went to retrieve battery cables. After inspecting my car, the man said that even if he jumped me, I would lose power down the road and would then be without help and possibly in a worse situation. He didn't feel right about charging me up and sending me on my way.

After listening to him, I felt what he was saying was true. There was no cell service where I was at but he had a landline that I could use to call my husband. My husband would need to come and rescue me and the car. We would need to wait there for him.

After making the phone call, Santa Claus offered us some ice cream. I said yes, and he brought us to the ice cream counter and proceeded to scoop out perfectly round balls of strawberry ice cream.

As he scooped up the ice cream, he started talking. His choice of topics shocked me. As he casually scooped the ice cream, he told me that sometimes, when bad things happen, people blame God.

"But what they don't realize," he said as he handed me the ice cream scooped into a cone, "was that God might have saved you from something else. You could have been hit by a deer or something else worse could have happened. God stepped in and said I'm going to stop your car to save you from something else."

He continued, "I talk to God all the time. He told me one morning to fill up my gas can. Later that day someone called me and after he said he needed help I told him, 'you don't need to tell me. God was thinking about you this morning and told me you would need help.' This man had recently lost his daughter and was angry at God. I told him, 'God is always thinking about you.'"

My head cocked, and I leaned in slightly as this man with a big white beard talked. I looked at him and thought, *Do you know God?* I wanted to ask him that blunt question but, instead, it came out more politely and less blunt, "Tell me about your relationship with God."

"I'm glad you said relationship. Relationship with God is what it's all about. If I have a relationship with someone, then I'll talk to Him all the time. I talk to God all the time."

I wanted him to keep talking. I didn't want him to stop, so I prodded him with another question, "In what way has God helped you in your life?"

"My daughter was raped. I should have killed the two men who did it. In fact, if they had come home that night I would have. I would have ended up like all those guys in prison. Not only that but it eats you up inside, thinking about what they did to her. According to the world, a real man would have gone after those men and done something to defend his family."

"How could you come back from something like that?" I prodded, wanting him to keep sharing his story.

The man raised his finger and pointed upward. "God," he said. "My relationship with God." He then picked up a cup. "You see this cup. If there's hatred and anger and junk in this cup, then God can't come in and fill it. We need to give it to Him and lay it at the feet of the cross." This man's eyes were turning red and misty as he spoke.

"How could you do that with something so big?" I asked him in amazement.

"Now I like to think that maybe what they did was worse than what I did, but I don't know that. I've hurt a lot of people too, and I need to recognize that I need mercy too."

"But how did you start forgiving those men? Did it take you years?"

"No, it didn't take years. It took months for God to take it from me. The memory is still there, but the pain is gone. Smells don't bother me anymore or places. It's all gone."

"How?" I asked.

"You start out by writing out on a piece of paper all the people who hurt you. Name them all. On the other side of the paper, you write all the people that you hurt. Now, I hurt a lot of people. I sold drugs and there were a lot of mothers and kids who went without food and stuff, but I didn't care as long as I got my fix. You wouldn't believe the man that I was. You wouldn't like me. I was a bad person. I hurt a lot of people."

He stopped for a second and let that thought hang in the air as he intently looked in my eyes. "You know God sent His Son, and He died for them just as much as He died for me." He then picked up the cup again, "This cup can't be full of hatred or I can't be given the mercy I need."

"Yes," I leaned into him a bit, "But what they did was so much worse than what you did. How do you get past that?"

"I don't know that. I've hurt other people badly too. It's just life. If you think you haven't hurt other people, you're blind and that's not right. You take your list and you throw it in the fire and give it to God."

"So, it's that simple?"

"I didn't say it was simple. Having a relationship with God isn't for the weak. It takes a lot of effort. Remember that God told us what to pray for." He then recited the simple but beautiful Lord's prayer. "You're supposed to pray for those that despitefully use you and persecute you. That is part of what we're supposed to do. When we start doing that, our heart changes. I kept working at it and over time, God took the poison out of my cup. And filled me with love and mercy. Now I wouldn't ever invite those men over for dinner, but it's a simple pray of 'God, send them goodness and help them.'

"And then God does something else; He sends people to you who need your help. Then you can help them get through what they're going through.

"I'll tell you this. When I get before my Maker I want Him to see His image in me. If it weren't because of Him, I would be in jail. He saved me. I need His mercy. So, I'm going to keep my glass clean and leave my hate at the foot of the cross."

I was thirstily drinking in all that he was saying. It was a powerful conversation for me and literally just blew my mind. First, that he could come through such trauma and be able to forgive and let go of the pain was a miracle in my mind. I was struggling to let go of the pain. He stood before me as one who had gone through what I had considered much worse and more difficult to let go. And he stood there healed and happy and no longer in pain. He could let go of the pain and be filled with light and goodness.

He gave me a lesson on what I called the double-sided coin. We're told we need to forgive and let go of what was done to us. We're told that forgiveness is more about us than those who hurt us. Forgiveness will bring us happiness and peace. But the other side of that coin is that we need forgiveness and mercy for the sins that we've committed. "Forgive our debts as we forgive our debtors." The double-sided coin.

What happens though is like what God described in the scriptures. The Pharisees were in a corner saying, "Thank God we're better than you and haven't committed these sins." And the other guy is in the corner smiting his chest, saying, "Oh God, have mercy on me, a sinner."

When we close our eyes to the reality that we sin and that we've hurt others, we're not acknowledging our need for a redeemer with the other side of the coin. Nor are we allowing the humility we need to enter in as we realize our TOTAL dependence on God and His mercy for our sins and for sins committed against us.

"How could you forgive? What they did was so much bigger than what you ever did?" I said.

"How do you know that?" He looked at me intently. "I've harmed women and children because I sold their husbands and dad's drugs. I didn't care. I just wanted my fix and my money. They suffered at my hand. Plus, how can I truly say I haven't hurt someone like they hurt me with my daughter? I mean, can we ever truly know that?"

My heart burned inside me and felt that all that he said was true. I needed that conversation at that time. The double-sided coin. Realizing that we're totally dependent on God to forgive and be forgiven. If you're justifying yourself and labeling your mistakes as not as bad, then you're destined to chase your tail and be spinning and stuck. I must do work on both sides of the coin.

The man continued, "We all think of sins as a labeling system, that some are worse than others and some are better. The fact is that all of them are sins and can keep us from God. There's only one sin that God said is unforgiveable and that is denying the Holy Ghost. The rest are forgivable. When we're working on forgiveness, it gets in our way when we try to label sins as worse or better. We mostly give ourselves the better end of the deal and not its full weight. We all equally need God's mercy if we can see it and realize it."

One of the important blessings of realizing that you're being shown mercy is that it helps you give up the "fight" for fairness. "Let God judge between me and thee." It allows you to mentally not think about it anymore. The fight for fairness keeps us stuck. You then start to put your mental space into productive healing ways. You let it go at Jesus's feet. Thinking about what was done against you doesn't help you nor does it help you see what mercy you've been given because you're then so focused on others and not yourself. The greatest place of peace is focusing on yourself. These other thoughts keep you spinning and measuring and spinning and comparing again, and that never ends up good.

This chapter was about the double-sided coin and how we need to look at both sides of the coin to get out of being stuck and seeking for quality of life. The next chapter, we'll look at what we can own.

YOUR ACTION PLAN

Journal:

- What are ways that you need mercy in your life?

Physical Action:

- Take a piece of paper and write on one side the people who have hurt you. Write down the names. Then I want you to write on the other side of the paper the names of the people whom you have hurt. When you do that, throw it into the fire and give it to God

Mental Action:

Repeat this affirmation morning and night:

God will pay the debt owed to me.

For the full list of affirmations, go to
https://beckyjonesbtcoach.com/freeactionguide

WHAT CAN I OWN?

I n my work with those who have suffered at the hands of betrayal trauma, I've seen that the other party dishes so much out on them that it becomes very heavy. So many of the things that someone will throw at you and want you to own really aren't yours to own. It's exhausting work to unravel what's your stuff and what's someone else's, especially for those who just want to please and not fight.

My shoulders felt heavy so often. I could physically feel a weight on my shoulders. But, after so much time sorting out the truth and lies and owning what was really mine and letting go of what wasn't, my shoulders began to ease up. I could feel physical relief.

You need to figure out what is yours to own and what isn't yours to own.

Owning things gave me power. As I saw things I could work on that were not related to my husband who betrayed me, it helped me to find who I was again and start owning who I am and who I want to be rather than just reacting to someone's treatment of me.

What could I own? What isn't mine to own?

Answering these questions will give you insights on the work that you need to still do. Finding ways that you can strengthen yourself, your talents, your connections with healthy people and with your Higher Power will keep you moving forward and staying unstuck in the betrayal trauma.

In this chapter, I reminded you to focus on what you can own and what you can fix. In the next chapter, we'll talk about forgiveness.

YOUR ACTION PLAN

Journal:

- Did I treat someone according to my own values or how they treated me?
- Did their behavior alter what I felt about myself or how I acted?
- Am I responding in the way that's true to who I want to be?
- Am I focusing too much on another's behaviors and not focusing on strengthening myself?
- What are my responsibilities in my life that are just mine and no one else's?

Physical Action:

Pour two different types of uncooked pasta into a bowl. Mix them together. Now, take the time to sort the two different types of pasta back into two separate piles of pasta. Notice the choice you have to make to sort the pasta. How is this similar to your life? Will it take an action on your part to sort out what is yours and what is not yours? What type of action would it take to sort those?

Mental Action:

Repeat this affirmation morning and night:

I can own my own stuff.

For the full list of affirmations, go to
https://beckyjonesbtcoach.com/freeactionguide

FORGIVENESS

I woke up to the sun shining, but inside my heart, the sun wasn't shining. I woke up realizing that today would be another day that I would have to work hard to push the anger out of my heart and forgive.

Forgiveness is like that Greek myth where the man was cursed to push the rock up the hill. Each day, he had to start over and push it back up the hill. Even if he reached the top of the hill that day, he was cursed to have to start over every morning. Forgiveness is like that. We work hard all day long, knowing that we need to forgive, only to wake up and have to do it all over again. Sometimes, it seems too hard and too exhausting.

I think forgiveness is like that in the beginning. But, if we're committed to the process of forgiveness and get up and work at it every day, with God's help, we can forgive and be free. One day, we'll go to bed and realize that we didn't have to push that rock up the hill that day. I believe that forgiveness isn't a one-and-done type deal. It's like exercises that make me into an athlete, but I still have to maintain that level of fitness to perform as an athlete would.

Forgiveness is defined in Wikipedia as "the intentional and voluntary process by which a victim undergoes a change in feelings and attitude regarding an offense, lets go of negative emotions such as vengefulness... [with] an increased ability to wish the offender well."[46]

---

[46] https://en.wikipedia.org/wiki/Forgiveness

Why forgive? Forgiveness, to me, frees up the energy you once put in blame or holding a grudge and allows you to use that energy for something better. You rediscover who you really are and who God made you to be.

How do you forgive?

1. To forgive you need to let go of blame for past hurt. Blaming will keep you stuck. Placing blame magnifies your pain. Blame keeps alive the hurt that otherwise might heal. Let it go. I know blame feels like a warm coat, but it's not. It's deceptive and full of holes. You'll never heal with blame. When a blaming thought comes into your mind, it's nurtured and cultivated. However, if you nurture blaming thoughts, it will keep alive the hurt that you feel and not allow it to heal.

2. Let go of your need to be validated. Let go of the need for people to see how you were wronged. Letting go of blame requires a great deal of humility. When we're humble, we can overcome hurt feelings and we can forgive others.

3. Take responsibility for the condition of your heart. You can't control what happens to you. But you can control how you respond to it.

One day, I got a call from a friend that my daughter had fallen off a horse and would need to be taken to the hospital. We took her to the hospital and found she had a few broken bones, some lacerations, and bruising. She got the wonderful care that she needed, and, after a time, the broken bones were able to heal, and the lacerations and bruising disappeared.

However, she kept complaining that her shoulder hurt. We took her in and an x-ray revealed that the bones had healed. It was determined that an MRI was necessary to see what was still ailing her. After getting the MRI, they discovered a very rare outcome: this twelve-year-old had torn her rotator cuff.

What followed were months of physical therapy for her and unexpected lessons from God for me.

I learned that bones heal on their own. You simply set them back in place, protect them, and, over time, those broken bones will heal.

It's not the same with a torn rotator cuff. It has to have a load to heal. Putting a load on a muscle looked like exercises that worked that specific muscle. My daughter was given an expert physical therapist who told her specific exercises to work that muscle so she could start the healing process. She was given the exercises that needed to be done to rebuild muscle fibers.

Initially, it was very painful for her to put a load on that torn rotator cuff. She could only do a few exercises at a time and those exercises were very painful.

Outside of physical therapy, my daughter struggled to do them. Why would she want to do something she knew was going to hurt? It took time and experience, her painfully pushing through the exercise with her physical therapist, and seeing that it was making a difference in her pain level and the functionality of her shoulder. She was getting better, and that inspired her to do the exercises on her own.

I learned so much during this time: lessons from my God as to what I needed to do. Like a broken bone, there were some things about my experience that would just heal on its own. I wouldn't need to do much after the talented and skilled doctor set the bone back in. I would have to deal with an inconvenient "cast" for a while but, for the most part, wouldn't have to do any work to heal that bone.

My heart however was a different story. It was a muscle. It needed a load to heal. It wouldn't just heal on its own. I needed to put a load on my torn heart, take responsibility for the condition of my heart, purify my heart, and learn to see others as God does. I couldn't change someone else's perspective, but I could change mine.

How do you put a load on a torn heart? What does that look like?

I credit all I learned on how to heal my torn heart to Mindee[47]

---

[47] "Summers, Melinda." LIFEstory Transformation. Accessed February 8, 2020. http://www.lifestorytransformation.com/summers-melinda.html.

1. Write down all that you see in the other person. All that you have labeled them to be: bad selfish, mean, dishonest. Get it out.
2. Then throw that away and bring out a new piece of paper. Write down just the opposite of the bad that you wrote and anything else you can think of.
3. Read it morning and night.

This is very hard. You might have to pray for help to do this.

This exercise eliminates some roadblocks of forgiveness. By changing my focus on what they did and what my experience with them was, I made it easier to change my heart and let go of the anger.

This exercise was miraculous for me. Doing that helped change things in me. I don't even know how to explain it. I learned by experience that changing my focus on what they did to me and how they treated me made it easier to forgive.

"And now behold, I ask of you…have ye spiritually been born of God? Have ye received his image in your countenances? Have ye experienced this mighty change in your hearts?"[48]

I believe forgiveness is a gift from God. It's God who really gives us the ability to forgive. He stands beside us and helps us loosen our grip upon anger and our appropriate need for justice and turn it over to Him. It requires a lot of faith and trust in Him. Faith and trust come as we study the word of God and the life of Christ. We realize that Christ knows betrayal. He knows rejection. He can help us to forgive.

I want to make an important point. Forgiveness isn't the same as reconciliation. Forgiveness is about one person: you, and it's between you and God. Reconciliation involves two people: you and the other person. Not everyone you forgive means that you'll be able to reconcile the relationship and have that relationship back in your life. They may not be safe. If we view forgiveness as reconciliation, you may not want to forgive! Fortunately, forgiveness doesn't mean reconciliation. Forgiveness doesn't

---

[48] "Alma 5:14." The Church of Jesus Christ of Latter-day Saints. Accessed February 8, 2020. https://www.churchofjesuschrist.org/study/scriptures/bofm/alma/5?lang=eng.

SEXUAL BETRAYAL SUCKS, BUT YOU GOT THIS.

mean no boundaries. In fact, with forgiveness, you probably have MORE boundaries to keep and sustain the forgiveness.

I know, for me, forgiveness can sometimes be discouraging. I think that I've got it in the bag and packed up and put on the shelf and marked as a "done" on my to-do list, but then something will happen and knock it off the shelf and down onto my lap.

I've, therefore, come to the conclusion that forgiveness is a continual process you work on all the time. You can't become complacent but must always work to give it to God.

But remember, this is what it would look like to "show up" every day (Brené Brown). It's going to get a little messy when you're working through things and not just hiding out. Give yourself that. Forgiveness might be something that shows up every now and again, even if you thought you had it boxed up and done. But as you get out into the world and show up and not just hide out, you'll find more layers to work through and things will come up that you had no idea existed inside you. But I try to not look at it as a bad thing. I like to look at it as a way to frequently cleanse myself and become more like my Heavenly Father and His Son Jesus Christ.

In this chapter, we talked about forgiveness. In the next chapter, we're going to talk about finding what you want. I talked about finding what you want at the beginning of this book and want to talk about it again because in each stage, we're finding out what we want after this betrayal.

YOUR ACTION PLAN

Journal:

- Do you feel like forgiveness is for you?
- In what way would forgiveness help your life?
- Do you feel discouraged with forgiveness, like it's an abstract concept you don't know how to grasp?
- Does what happened to you hold you back in your life?
- What does it look like to take responsibility for the condition of your heart?

Physical Action:

- Write down all that you see in the other person. All that you have labeled them to be: bad, selfish, mean, dishonest. Get it out.
- Then throw that away and bring out a new piece of paper. Write down just the opposite of the bad that you wrote and anything else you can think of.
- Read it morning and night.
- Try this for one week and journal about what the experience was like for you.

Mental Action:

Repeat this affirmation morning and night:

I can forgive.

For the full list of affirmations, go to
https://beckyjonesbtcoach.com/freeactionguide

FINDING WHAT YOU WANT

In sexual betrayal, it's so exhausting to sift through the countless opinions that come your way and figure out what you want. So many voices and perspectives compete for your attention. It's difficult to feel centered. On top of that, your own pain is telling you stuff. It's like the hash of food on your plate on Thanksgiving day, where all the food is packed so closely together on your plate that you can't tell one dish from another.

In figuring out what you want, I want to make two points. First, your intuition will help you know what to do. Polishing and oiling your intuition "genie lamp" will yield great benefits such as confidence in your path. Secondly, reaching out to your Higher Power is important. Tapping into that source of power in your life will yield insight, strength, and foresight.

One of the most important points I tell my clients is that your inner voice is your greatest gift. You may not be confident in what your intuition is telling you or have the courage to follow it, but it's still there guiding you. One of my roles as a betrayal trauma coach is to help you see what your intuition is telling you and then have the courage to follow it.

We can find what we want by dreaming and exploring in a safe place and seeing how that feels. It's like being in a clothing shop, trying on clothes. Others hand you clothing to try on and you say, "No, I don't like how it looks on me." Or you may say, "Yes! This feels good." It's just like that but instead of playing with clothes, we play with our emotions, our boundaries, and questions we have about what we need to do.

Pay close attention to how you feel and that will teach you a lot about what you should do. That awareness of how your body feels when you "try" things teaches you so much! As you work on this daily to watch yourself and your emotions, you'll be led to what you should do by yourself. That's as real and organic as it gets.

Reaching out to your Higher Power is crucial. The voice of God is unmanufactured. You cannot manufacture your own peace or enlightenment. A belief I have is that God will speak to me. God can and will guide me. That's a foundational belief. I know if I ask, He will help me. He will guide me. He will speak to me. My purpose is to remind you that He is there, and He will speak to you.

Sometimes, it's hard to recognize that you were given what you asked for. Just as quickly as the agony came, it was gone. You feel better but you forget the direct correlation between kneeling down in prayer before your Higher Power and then standing up and feeling peace. My confidence in my Higher Power grew when I recognized when the change happened and when my mood changed. Being aware of how God answered, helped me grow in confidence, and I sought Him out more.

I remember a few times when I would feel a burst of enlightenment or peace and I stopped and said to myself, "That's it. That was it, Becky." I've trained horses, and if you've ever trained a horse, you look for ways that the horse gives you a release. A release from a horse is when you see them listen or do what you ask. It's much like that with me. All of a sudden, I would get that release and realize that what I was doing or thinking at the time was right. That could guide me. Then I'm more apt to look for it next time and see it for what it is.

As I started looking for His voice, I was listening more to what I needed. I needed help. Help to see past my current situations. I needed help to discern the opinions being thrown at me. I needed help to cope with the pain that I felt. I needed help to cope with the pain that came because others wanted someone to blame or couldn't cope themselves, and, somehow, weirdly, they took it out on me.

My belief and experience is that God is good and faithful. If you search for Him, you'll find Him. He never leaves a cry for help unanswered. Never stop asking. Never stop praying. Never stop searching for answers. If you're struggling to believe He will help or answer, tell Him that. If you're struggling with anger, tell Him that. If you're struggling to trust Him, tell Him that. If you need help to understand something, ask Him for understanding. As you keep reaching out to Him, you'll come to know that He's there. There's a God in heaven, who is your heavenly Father, and that He is keenly aware of you.

I think that this is a beautiful and valuable rock. I picked up this rock and put it in my pocket because I realized as I started walking down this road, that there was no way I could navigate this path on my own. What a priceless pebble that I put in my pocket. God is there with me walking this path.

In this chapter, we talked about how listening and following your intuition and connecting to your Higher Power will help you figure out what you want. In the next chapter, I'll share my thoughts about your value.

YOUR ACTION PLAN

Journal:

- What are other people telling you to do? How do they feel you should handle your situation?
- What pressures do you feel about how you should handle your situation?
- What are your beliefs about your Higher Power? Do you feel like He will speak to you? What is your method of connecting with Him?

Physical Action:

- Play the old-fashioned game of telephone where you take a tin can and a string and have a conversation between you and someone else. What do you notice about your conversation? Are you able to hear each other clearly? How do you feel like your perspective on life changes what you hear and say? How does the other person's perspective on life change what they say and hear? To make the communication better between you two, what can you do differently?

Mental Action:

Repeat these affirmations morning and night:

I can know what I need.
I can know what I want.
I know how to take care of myself.

For the full list of affirmations, go to
https://beckyjonesbtcoach.com/freeactionguide

MY VALUE

Never would I have guessed that through a terrible trial, I would come to know something I hadn't known since I was young: my value.

When I was a teenager, I would recite a poem with other kids each week. "We're children of God who loves us, and we love Him." Not only would we recite every week, but we were told weekly, in lessons and in conversations, that we were so important and valuable. We were told we were children of God.

I would hear this, but then I would go to high school where no one would pay attention to me, where most people didn't reach out to me. I had to reach out to them. I would hear this but felt so much pressure to perform perfectly in sports. The praise didn't come unless I did well. I would hear this but felt pressure in school to study hard and prove how smart I was and to serve and go, go, go. I would feel guilty when I took any rest and relaxation time for myself.

Out in the big, bad world, how was I supposed to know I was valuable? Value was based on performance, looks, and praise. It was a hard concept for me to believe that my value just existed. If I were valuable, why did I have to work so hard to see it? How could no one else see it? Praise came when I did stuff right. Disappointment came when I did stuff wrong. I learned very quickly that I needed to be perfect to maintain my value. My value seemed to ebb and flow with what I did. And to top it off, I thought I must be really bad if it takes a God to see and know my value.

As a youth, these thoughts ran through my mind daily. I didn't know my value. I saw my value connected to how people viewed me. Because of that, I wasn't able to voice my opinions or what I thought very well because I wanted their approval. It was a very shaky foundation. I was so used to silencing my own desires, thinking it the noble, peacemaking thing to do. To make matters worse, when I finally needed to voice my opinion, it came out unfiltered, desperate, harsh, and unkind. To this day, I'm still working on being able to stand in a solid place of being confident, to say what I think and not be afraid to speak how I feel. And, to do so calmly and confidently, without fear of others disagreeing with me.

I didn't believe I was valuable. I saw that I was only valuable in what I did. I felt so worthless that only God could really see it. I craved attention. I craved validation. I needed others to see my worth. I needed others people's praise like food. When I didn't get it, I was shaky and unconfident. When I did get it, it was like a cream Twinkie that tastes amazing but the sugar buzz burned off quickly, leaving me wanting more.

I lacked the ability to give myself what I so desperately wanted others to give to me. I expected others to give me what I couldn't give to myself.

I sensed what I lacked deep down inside of me but I didn't know how to fix it. I worked hard on my connection with God. I tried to have faith that I was valuable to Him. Logically, I knew that if Jesus died for me, then I must hold some value. But it was hard to feel it. I couldn't grasp it in my soul. Sometimes, it would come but it was fleeting and didn't stay.

I struggled with the pull between my value and what I did. I did a lot but I couldn't always sustain it, so when I couldn't, that lesser feeling would come back. I struggled then to feel enough when I couldn't output more. I was destined to run myself ragged chasing value, approval, validation, and confidence.

Then when something so huge as sexual betrayal hits your life, everything is shattered. You're staring at shards of glass littering the floor that have no possibility of being put back together. I'm fighting that inward feeling that what I thought all along was true.

However, the beautiful thing that actually happened was that God took those broken pieces on the floor and He said "I'm putting you back together in a way that's stronger than ever before. I'll heal you of all those mistaken ideas and lies that you believed."

God said He would put me back together again. In my naivety in thinking I knew how God thinks, I thought He would use those very same pieces and somehow find a way to rearrange them perfectly again in the very same way. But that wasn't God's plan for me. He started building me anew. Fortunately, I was so broken, I let Him. I didn't fight anything but humbly let Him guide me and direct me, and I listened to everything. I didn't fight anymore against what I thought was right. I didn't keep spinning the same silly logic about why I did what I did. Everything was shattered on the ground. He wasn't going to put those pieces glued back in the right order. He was leaving it there and building something from other material.

What other material? This time, it was built on truth, pure principles, and revelation straight from God in such a powerful way I couldn't deny it. I started to see the lies I had bought into that changed my perspective about myself. I saw the lies that allowed me to treat others differently than what their divine nature deserved. I saw lies that kept me in darkness. But somehow, light was pouring in and I started to see. He was building me back up based on truth.

Mindee, that wonderful counselor, gave me an amazing example of a water bottle. We go through life and we fill a water bottle with junk: rocks and dirty water. How can good, clean, pure water be poured in unless we take out the junk first?

The truth I saw more clearly was my sandy foundations: other people's weaknesses don't reflect my value. Their inability to love me and see me for who I was and their judgment of me wasn't my value.

Other people's lenses aren't truth. Truth comes with a witness from the spirit. Truth is how things really are, how they were and how they are to come. Now, if I can feel the spirit in what they say, then I know what they're saying is true. But their perspective, no matter how confidently given, doesn't constitute law.

I began to separate myself from others. I began to cut those strings that allowed their treatment of me to affect how I felt about myself. I started to be confident in what I felt and knew despite others having a different opinion.

So, my question to you is this: What lies have you believed about yourself because of someone else's behavior?

It may take days, months, or even years to empty your personal "water bottle" of the lies you believed about yourself that weren't true because of someone else's behavior. But do it, get it out, and look at it for what it is, lies and untruth.

What do I know now?

I have an undeniable belief in my value as a human being, as a woman. I have confidence in myself. I believe now that God put everything in me that I needed to be successful. I truly love and value myself. I treat myself with the respect I deserve. I love myself and give mercy and compassion to myself.

And with that strong view myself, it's a natural process that those around me will have to step into that same space in order to be in my life. Those who treat me with the same love and respect that I give myself will be allowed to stay; otherwise, they'll need to go.

In this chapter, we talked about my value. In the next chapter, we'll talk about healing.

YOUR ACTION PLAN

Journal:

- What have you believed about yourself because of someone else's behavior?
- Was there a time in your life that you saw your value? When was that?
- When did you start to not see your value?

Physical Action:

- Take an empty water bottle and put in rocks and sand and dirty water. Now, try pouring in clean, fresh water. What happens to the dirt? How much clean water can you get in?
- Now take that water bottle that has the dirt and the sand and the dirty water and dump that out. After you dump out the dirt and sand, pour in the clean water. How much clean water can you get in?
- What is the difference between these two methods on how much clean water you can get into the water bottle? Why is there a difference? How can you apply that to your life?

Mental Action:

Repeat these affirmations morning and night:

I am so awesome.
I am amazing.
I have everything I need inside myself to be successful.

For the full list of affirmations, go to
https://beckyjonesbtcoach.com/freeactionguide

HEALING

The Bible talks about a woman healed from an issue of blood by touching Christ's garment.[49] She had this malady for 12 years and spent all her money trying to find out what was wrong.

What an amazing gift for her to be healed personally by Christ. God gave her an incredible moment after all those grueling years.

We know she had faith and courage because she spent all her money trying to find a solution, to find something to help her. I picture her hunting down every lead that someone suggested. She searched feverishly to be healed. We know she had faith because she was in tune with God and was led by Him to the very spot she needed to be.

God could have healed her with anything. He could have made any of those work for her. But instead, He had a special gift in store for her. He healed her personally.

It couldn't have come earlier. It was in the perfect moment of time. Christ was in His ministry.

You know she was close to God and hadn't given up on God or His timing. She was willing to be patient with God and trust His timing. She was in tune with God. That day, she was guided on where to go and where

---

[49] "Matthew 9." The Church of Jesus Christ of Latter-day Saints. Accessed February 8, 2020. https://www.churchofjesuschrist.org/study/scriptures/nt/matt/9.20?lang=eng&clang=eng#p19.

SEXUAL BETRAYAL SUCKS, BUT YOU GOT THIS.

to be. It wasn't a coincidence. She was trusting and listening to God all the time. He told her where to go and where to be.

She didn't give up on God. She didn't become tired because nothing was working out. She was ever trusting as God worked His plan in her life.

And how much God loved her to give her that special individualized experience with Christ. And her testimony was sure: the power of God over anything that man can provide. That knowledge could only come after the right amount of time and experience with other things. God in His wisdom arranges everything.

This insight came to me after I felt so discouraged. I know God has all power. Why wasn't He healing me? It's so hard to be patient when you're in so much pain.

But then it came… the grace that I recognized was His to give and only comes from God. Strength and perspective and peace. Pure peace. Pure strength to rise above it and be more like Christ. Pure strength to push aside the offenses and pain that so easily come from others. Pure perspective that powers the strength. God's view of it all that lifts you above the pain.

The words came to mind, "Remember, I said I would heal you. Remember I said I would heal you. Regardless of what anyone else does, I am focused on healing you."

My testimony to you is to not give up on God. He will heal you. Don't give up on the healing that's yours to receive. He went through so much to give us the gift of healing. He can give it to you. Trust in that. He wants to heal you.

YOUR ACTION PLAN

Journal:

- Are there any similarities to your life and the story of the woman in the Bible being healed by the issue of blood?
- Do you feel discouraged that you haven't been healed from betrayal trauma? In what areas of your life do you feel like you lack healing?
- In what areas of your life have you felt healing from betrayal trauma? Journal about how far you've come and what needs you still have.

Physical Action:

- Find a stream of water. Sit by it. Now put your hand into the water. Think about how Jesus Christ is compared to living water. Imagine that by dipping your hand into the water, you're healed. While you sit there, think about how in your life you can "reach" for Jesus Christ. Are you actively "reaching" for Jesus Christ or do you just sit there hoping for healing? What are ways you can "reach" out to Him?

Mental Action:

Repeat these affirmations morning and night:

God will heal me.
I can be healed.
God wants to heal me.

For the full list of affirmations, go to
https://beckyjonesbtcoach.com/freeactionguide

EPILOGUE

I wrestled with writing this book. It was super scary, and I very vulnerable. Up until this point, very few people knew that I did betrayal trauma coaching.

However, I don't feel it's coincidence that I have a desire inside me to help others navigate the trauma that comes with sexual betrayal.

It was a sacred experience for me to be snatched out of the gall of bitterness and pain because of the great love and mercy of my Father in Heaven and Savior, Jesus Christ. I feel similar to those who were healed by the Savior and went back to the village and shared what good things the Lord did for them. Because of that, it's my desire to bear my witness and testimony that He lives! He loves me! He saved me!

So, in the end, this book wasn't about me and my fears or about people knowing what other job I did for a living. It was about what was placed in my heart by God.

A certain boy had five loaves and five fishes. He was approached to give those loaves and fishes to feed others. I'm assuming he had huge doubts as to what good it would do in the midst of so much need; however, he gave it. Likewise, I have doubts but know that I've been asked to give; therefore, I give what I have.

Sexual betrayal sucks but you got this. You can do this. Keep searching for what you need and just like manna was given to the children of Israel day by day, you'll be given what you need as well: day by day.

My testimony is that God our Father lives and loves us. His Son, our Savior Jesus Christ lives and loves us too. He is the Great Jehovah. He is the Redeemer. He came to pay my debts and the debts owed to me. He saved me. He healed me. He restored me.

ABOUT THE AUTHOR

Betrayal Trauma and Affair Recovery Coach: Becky Jones

My role as a Betrayal trauma and affair recovery coach is to help you stay unstuck in your recovery and keep you moving forward. I walk side by side with you as you navigate the heart-breaking betrayal that just landed in your lap. I coach you on how to deal with powerful emotions, understand how to set boundaries, understand practices of self-care, disconnecting from the lies you believed about yourself because of your partner's behavior, finding your voice, speaking your truth, and so much more.

Two dominate values that guide my work as a coach:

1. You have a light inside you. That light will always tell you truth and guide you to truth. As a betrayal trauma coach, I don't give you any answers but I help you discover what your body and that light is already telling you. My job as a betrayal trauma coach is to help you see that light inside you and guide you to the courage to follow it.

2. I believe people are powerful. As a betrayal trauma coach, I want to help you disconnect from the lies or behavior of others and emerge from this betrayal stronger, more confident, owning what is only yours to own, and finally unabashedly speaking your feelings and perspective.

Outside of Coaching: I'm the mother of 7 children, an avid book reader, a wanna-be mountain biker, a lover of good food, and if I'm being really vulnerable, I'm sort of obsessed with the royals and want to go to England someday.

My Credentials:

- Betrayal trauma coach for Bloom for Women
- You Bloom Program Coach
- Public speaker in the area of betrayal trauma recovery
- Author of *Sexual Betrayal Sucks but You Got This.* and *A Little Tent in the Woods.*

NEED HELP?

I f you would like betrayal trauma coaching from me, you can find me in two places. I coach both men and women through trauma that comes with sexual betrayal:

1. **bloomforwomen.com**- Addo Recovery's Bloom for Women.
   o I do individual and group betrayal trauma coaching for their Bloom for Women program. It's awesome and you'll find a wonderful community and a wealth of resources at your fingertips. They are AMAZING!
   o I also am a program manager for their You Bloom program.

2. **beckyjonesbtcoach.com**- My website.
   o You can find me on my website. You can schedule individual coaching sessions with me there.

Reach out if you have any further book topics you would like me to delve into: beckyjonesauthor@gmail.com

Reach out to me if you would like to schedule coaching sessions with me. becky@beckyjonesbtcoach.com

BIBLIOGRAPHY

"5 Factors That Make You Feel Shame." *Psychology Today.* Sussex Publishers. Accessed February 8, 2020. https://www.psychologytoday.com/us/blog/science-choice/201510/5-factors-make-you-feel-shame.

"Alma 5:14." The Church of Jesus Christ of Latter-day Saints. Accessed February 8, 2020. https://www.churchofjesuschrist.org/study/scriptures/bofm/alma/5?lang=eng.

Amazon. Accessed February 8, 2020. https://www.amazon.com/Becky-Jones/e/B0779R8QQH/ref=dp_byline_cont_ebooks_1.

Bayes-Fleming, Nicole, Grace Bullock, Barry Boyce, Crystal Goh, Kira M. Newman, and Linda Graham. "Getting Started with Mindfulness." Mindful, September 14, 2018. https://www.mindful.org/meditation/mindfulness-getting-started/.

Beattie, Melody. *Language of Letting Go.* Place of publication not identified: Hay House Inc, 2005.

Brown, Brené. "The Power of Vulnerability." TED. Accessed February 8, 2020. https://www.ted.com/talks/brene_brown_the_power_of_vulnerability?language=en.

Counselor, James E. FaustSecond. "The Healing Power of Forgiveness." The Church of Jesus Christ of Latter-day Saints. Accessed February 8, 2020. https://www.churchofjesuschrist.org/study/general-conference/2007/04/the-healing-power-of-forgiveness?lang=eng.

"Doctrine and Covenants 6:33." The Church of Jesus Christ of Latter-day Saints. Accessed February 8, 2020. https://www.churchofjesuschrist. org/study/scriptures/dc-testament/dc/6?lang=eng.

"Dr. Dr. Kevin Skinner, LMFT, CSAT, EMDR, Marriage & Family Therapist, Lindon, UT, 84042." *Psychology Today.* Sussex Publishers, July 20, 2019. https://www.psychologytoday.com/us/therapists/ dr-kevin-skinner-and-addo-recovery-lindon-ut/285636.

"Elizabeth Smart (@elizabeth_smart_official) • Instagram Photos and Videos." Instagram. Accessed February 8, 2020. https://www.instagram. com/elizabeth_smart_official/?hl=en.

"Eric Mikkelsen - Central Idaho Counseling 125 Commerce St Mccall, ID Marriage & Family Counselors." MapQuest. Accessed February 8, 2020. https://www.mapquest.com/us/idaho/eric-mikkelsen-central-idaho-counseling-351186811.

"Ether 12:37." The Church of Jesus Christ of Latter-day Saints. Accessed February 8, 2020. https://www.churchofjesuschrist.org/study/scriptures/ bofm/ether/12?lang=eng.

Eyring, Henry B. "Creating Peace: Blessed Are the Peacemakers." BYU Speeches. Accessed February 8, 2020. https://speeches.byu.edu/talks/ henry-b-eyring/blessed-peacemakers/.

"Family and Marriage Counselors." Reviews - McCall, ID. Accessed February 8, 2020. https://www.healthgrades.com/providers/eric-mikkelsen-xyln82h.

"Forgiveness." Wikipedia. Wikimedia Foundation, January 30, 2020. https://en.wikipedia.org/wiki/Forgiveness.

Henley, William Ernest. "Invictus by William Ernest Henley." Poetry Foundation. Poetry Foundation. Accessed February 8, 2020. https:// www.poetryfoundation.org/poems/51642/invictus.

"Home." Partner Hope. Accessed February 8, 2020. https://partnerhope.com/.

"Homepage." Bloom for Women. Accessed February 8, 2020. https:// bloomforwomen.com/.

"How Do I Manage My Anger & Rage?" Bloom for Women, November 17, 2017. https://bloomforwomen.com/how-do-i-manage-my-anger-rage/.

"How Firm a Foundation." The Church of Jesus Christ of Latter-day Saints. Accessed February 8, 2020. https://www.churchofjesuschrist.org/manual/hymns/how-firm-a-foundation?lang=eng.

"Isaiah 49." The Church of Jesus Christ of Latter-day Saints. Accessed February 8, 2020. https://www.churchofjesuschrist.org/study/scriptures/ot/isa/49?lang=eng.

"Isaiah 61." The Church of Jesus Christ of Latter-day Saints. Accessed February 8, 2020. https://www.churchofjesuschrist.org/study/scriptures/ot/isa/61?lang=eng.

"Jesus Heals a Man Born Blind." Jesus Heals a Man Born Blind -. Accessed February 8, 2020. https://www.churchofjesuschrist.org/bible-videos/videos/jesus-heals-a-man-born-blind?lang=eng.

Katie, Byron, and Stephen Mitchell. *Loving What Is: Four Questions That Can Change Your Life*. New York: Harmony Books, 2002.

Lincoln, n.d.

"Luke 10." The Church of Jesus Christ of Latter-day Saints. Accessed February 8, 2020. https://www.churchofjesuschrist.org/study/scriptures/nt/luke/10.33?lang=eng&clang=eng#p32.

"Matthew 9." The Church of Jesus Christ of Latter-day Saints. Accessed February 8, 2020. https://www.churchofjesuschrist.org/study/scriptures/nt/matt/9.20?lang=eng&clang=eng#p19.

Maxwell, Neal A. "'Meek and Lowly' - Neal A. Maxwell." BYU Speeches. Accessed February 8, 2020. https://speeches.byu.edu/talks/neal-a-maxwell/meek-lowly/.

"Mindfulness." Dictionary.com. Dictionary.com. Accessed February 8, 2020. https://www.dictionary.com/browse/mindfulness.

"Moroni 10." The Church of Jesus Christ of Latter-day Saints. Accessed February 8, 2020. https://www.churchofjesuschrist.org/study/scriptures/bofm/moro/10.4-5?lang=eng.

Nelson, Russell M. "'Blessed Are the Peacemakers.'" The Church of Jesus Christ of Latter-day Saints. Accessed February 8, 2020. https://www.churchofjesuschrist.org/study/general-conference/2002/10/blessed-are-the-peacemakers?lang=eng.

"Peace." The Church of Jesus Christ of Latter-day Saints. Accessed February 8, 2020. https://www.churchofjesuschrist.org/study/manual/true-to-the-faith/peace.html?lang=eng#title1.

"Personal Boundaries." Wikipedia. Wikimedia Foundation, January 29, 2020. https://en.wikipedia.org/wiki/Personal_boundaries#cite_note-1.

"Personal Boundaries." Wikipedia. Wikimedia Foundation, January 29, 2020. https://en.wikipedia.org/wiki/Personal_boundaries#cite_note-1.

"Prana - Betrayal Trauma." Bloom for Women. Accessed February 8, 2020. https://bloomforwomen.com/prana-program/.

Rasband, Ester. *The Promise of the Atonement: Cure for Broken Dreams.* Springville, UT: Cedar Fort, 2005.

Richo, David. *How to Be an Adult: a Handbook on Psychological and Spiritual Integration.* Mahwah, NJ: Paulist Press, 2018.

Robison, Becca. "Freedom: The Dignity of Our Own Choice." Small Seed. July 24, 2017. https://www.thesmallseed.com/blog/2017/07/freedom-the-dignity-of-our-own-choice.

"Seeing Green: Jill Thomas." Seeing Green | Jill Thomas | Inspiration. Accessed February 8, 2020. https://www.churchofjesuschrist.org/inspiration/latter-day-saints-channel/watch/series/hope-works/seeing-green-jill-thomas-hope-works?lang=eng.

"Shame." Dictionary.com. Dictionary.com. Accessed February 8, 2020. https://www.dictionary.com/browse/shame.

"Summers, Melinda." LIFEstory Transformation. Accessed February 8, 2020. http://www.lifestorytransformation.com/summers-melinda.html.

Swensen, Jason. "'He Was in Charge': Richard Norby on Surviving Brussels Bombing through Faith in Jesus Christ." *Church News,* February 26, 2019. https://www.thechurchnews.com/members/2019-02-26/general-conference-rirchard-norby-terrorist-attacks-on-surviving-brussels-bombing-moving-forward-with-faith-in-jesus-christ-4477.

"Understanding Betrayal Trauma." Partner Hope, April 4, 2019. https://partnerhope.com/2016/11/understanding-betrayal-trauma/.

"What Is Betrayal Trauma." Dr. Jill Manning. Accessed February 8, 2020. https://drjillmanning.com/betrayal-trauma/.

"Why the Codependency Model Is Harmful to You | Betrayal Trauma Recovery." YouTube. Accessed February 8, 2020. https://youtu.be/epzxsrDp8kM.

"Yoga Therapy; Betrayal Trauma and Addiction Recovery." Sariah Bastian. Accessed February 8, 2020. https://www.sariahbastian.com/.

THANK YOU FOR READING THIS BOOK!

Every review matters, and it matters a *lot!*
Head over to Amazon or wherever you purchased
this book to leave an honest review for me.
Thank you SO much!
Your review helps me get my message out to others
that Sexual betrayal sucks, but you got this.

Made in the USA
Las Vegas, NV
21 May 2021